Basic Gas Turbines *for Helicopter Pilots*

About this Publication

Title:

Basic Gas Turbines

Series:

For Helicopter Pilots

Edition:

First published 1998, Seventh Edition, January 2022

Principal Author:

Mike Becker, ATPL(H), FIR, FER, Diploma (Training and Assessment)

Editor:

Bev Austen, BTech(CompSt), MEd(DTL)

Copyright

Copyright © 2022 Becker Helicopter Services Pty Ltd

Photos and Illustrations

The majority of photos and illustrations in this document have been sourced from Becker Helicopter Services Pty Ltd. The remainder is taken from the internet from various sources; Every effort has been made to ensure images with Creative Commons Licences have been used and appropriate attribution provided.

Disclaimer

Nothing in this text supersedes any operational documents issued by any civil aviation authority or regulatory body, aircraft, engine, and avionics manufacturers, or the operators of aircraft throughout the world. No responsibility is taken for the interpretation and application of the information contained in this document. Managing the safety of the aircraft is the sole responsibility of the pilot-in-command.

Every possible effort has been made to establish the accuracy of the information contained in this book, however, the author, Becker Helicopter Services Pty Ltd, accept no responsibility for errors or omissions.

The Publisher and the Author make no representations or warranties for the accuracy or completeness of the contents of this work and specifically disclaim all warranties, including without limitation warranties of fitness for a particular purpose. No warranty may be created or extended by sales or promotional materials. The advice and strategies contained herein may not be suitable for every situation. This work is sold with the understanding that the author is not engaged in rendering legal, accounting, or other professional services. If professional assistance is required, the services of a competent professional person should be sought. Neither the Publisher nor the Author shall be liable for damages arising therefrom.

The fact that an organisation or website is referred to in this work as a citation and/or a potential source of further information does not mean that the author or the Publisher endorses the information the organisation or website may provide or recommendations it may make. Further, readers should be aware that internet websites listed in this work may have changed or disappeared between when this work was written and when it is read.

Contents

About this Publication 1
Contents 2
About this Book 6
About the Author 7

Brief History 8
    Replacement of the Piston Engine by the Turbine Engine 8

Basic Jet Propulsion Principles 10
        Reaction principle 10
        Summary 10
    Gas Laws 11
        Charles' Law 11
        Boyle's Law 11
        Gay–Lussac's Law 11
        Combined Gas Law 12
        Summary 12
    Types of Jet Engine 12
    Rocket Jet 12
    Ram-jet 13
    Pulse-jet 13
    Turbine Jet 15
    Turbofans 15
        Turbofan engines can be either High bypass or low bypass 16
        High bypass 17
        Low bypass 17
        Low bypass with mixed exhaust 18
        Rear fan and Prop fan 18
    Turboprops 19
        Free power turbine schematic 20
        Fixed shaft power turbine schematic 20
    Turboshaft 21

How a Turbine Engine Works 22
    The way the engines work are different 22
    The Brayton Cycle 23
    Pressure, Volume, Velocity and Temperature 25
        Pressure Changes 25
        Volume (Velocity) Changes 25
        Temperature Changes 26
    Ducting 27
    Summary 27

Air Intake and Filters 28
        Fixed Wing 28
        Helicopters 28
    Intake Design 28
    Intake Ice 29
    Intake Filters 29
        Particle Separator 29
        Inlet Barrier Filter (IBF) 30

Compressor Section 31

Pressure Ratio	33
Centrifugal Compressor	33
Centrifugal Compressor: Impeller	34
Centrifugal Compressor: Diffuser	35
Centrifugal Compressor: Manifold	35
Axial Flow Compressor	36
Axial Flow Compressor: Cascade Effect	36
Axial Flow Compressor: Rotor Blades	38
Compressor rotor blade attachment	38
Stagger angle	39
Axial Flow Compressor: Stator Vanes	39
Combined Axial and Centrifugal Compressor	40
Airflow through the Engine	41
Airflow Control	42
Variable Inlet Guide Vanes	42
Variable Stator Vanes	43
Bleed Air Valve	43
Bleed air for accessories	45
Compressor Stalls and Surging	46
Symptoms of compressor stall or surge	48
Remedy for a compressor stall	48
Damage due to compressor stalls	49

Combustion Section — 50

Flame out	53
Types of Combustion Chamber	53
Can or Multiple-Can	53
Annular	54
Advantages of the annular type	54
A disadvantage of the annular type	54
Can-Annular	54
Multiple can-annular combustion chambers	55

Turbine Section — 56

Nozzle Guide Vanes (NGVs)	59
Rotating Turbine	59
Turbine Blade Types	60
Impulse turbine blade	60
Reaction turbine blade	60
Combined effect	61
Forces on a Turbine Blade	62
Blade shrouds	62
Blade attachment	62
Turbine blade materials	63
Turbine creep	63
Cooling of the Turbine Section	65
Internal air flow cooling	65
Surface film cooling	65
Combination convection and surface cooling	66

Accessory Drive Section — 67

Exhaust Section — 69

Gas Flow	70
Noise Suppression	71

  Noise suppression in helicopters 71
  Levels in Decibels 71

Fuel Control Systems in a Turbine Engine 72

 Electric Fuel Boost Pumps 73
 Engine Driven Fuel Pumps 74
 Fuel Control Unit (FCU) and Governors 75
  Governor 79
   B206 Collective "beep" Control 79
   B206 Linear Actuator 80
   Power Turbine Governor in the B206 80
 Electronic Engine Control Systems 81
  Electronic Engine Control (EEC) 81
  Fuel Flow Regulator (FFR) 81
  Full Authority Digital Engine Control (FADEC) 81
  Full Authority Fuel Control (FAFC) 81
  Data Acquisition Unit (DAU) 81
 Fuel Spray Nozzles 82
  Simplex 83
  Duplex 83
  Plumbing 84

Turbine Engine Fuel 85

 Fuel Types 85
 Turbine Fuel Characteristics 86
  Fuels are coloured for identification 86
  Types of Jet Fuel 86
  Comparison chart between AVGAS and AVTUR 87
 Water in Turbine Fuel 87
  Suspended Water 87
  Free Water 88
  Dissolved Water 88
  Testing for Water 89
  Ice in Turbine Fuel 89
  Heating Systems 90
  Fuel System Icing Inhibitor (FSII) 90
 Fuel Contamination 90

Turbine Engine Lubrication 91

 Functions of Oil 91
  Reduces Friction 91
  Provides Cooling 91
  Acts as a Sealant 91
  Protection against Corrosion 91
  Cleans 91
 Types of Engine Oil 92
  Straight Mineral Oil 92
  Metallic Ash Detergent Oil 92
  Ashless Dispersant Oil 92
  Synthetic Oil 92
  Compatibility 92
 Engine Oil Properties 93
  Viscosity 93

  Oil Grades 93
  Flash Point 93
  Pour Point... 93
  Chemical Stability 93
 Oils for Turbine Engines 93
 Turbine Engine Lubrication System 94
  Pressure Relief Valve System (PRV).. 95
  Full Flow System 95
  Components 95
   Oil tank and de-aerator 95
   Oil filter... 95
   Oil cooler 95
   Plumbing 96
   Oil pump.. 96
   Pressure relief valves for protection 96
   Chip detectors 97

Turbine Engine Sealing.. 98
  Types of seals 98
 Labyrinth Seals.. 98
 Carbon Seals... 99
 Ring Seals 99
 Hydraulic Seals.. 99
 Brush Seals 99

Turbine Engine Starting, Ignition and Shutdown 100
 Starter System... 100
  Basic Starting Components.. 101
   Starter motor 101
   Battery... 101
 Ignition System 102
  Ignition Components 102
   Igniter plug 102
   Igniter box 103
   Igniter leads or harness 103
 Starting Problems.. 104
  Hot Starts 104
  Hung Starts 104
  Wet Start 104
  Engine Relight 105
  Engine Shutdown 105
  Hot Shutdown.. 106

BGT Terminology... 107

Bibliography 114

Index 116

About this Book

Ten years in writing, this informative and easy to read aviation theory book on the workings of the helicopter turbine engine is a must for any pilot planning to convert to a turbine helicopter. With the learning pilot in mind. it provides graphic details of how the turbine engine works in a helicopter, how to operate a turbine engine, and how to cope with some of the problems you may encounter when operating this type of helicopter.

"Basic Gas Turbines for Helicopter Pilots" is written by Captain Mike Becker, one of Australia's most experienced helicopter instructors. With over 16,000 flight hours, and recipient of the "Captain John Ashton Award for Flight Standards and Aviation Safety" by the Guild of Air Pilots and Air Navigators of London, Mike's experience provides invaluable insights and real hands-on knowledge.

Mike Becker has been operating a helicopter flight school since 1995. As Chief Pilot and Head of Training Operations, Mike has managed and operated a fleet of over 20 helicopters while employing a team of more than 30 instructors to deliver over 10,000 turbine training hours per year.

This theory book converts all this experience into a practical, hands-on guide. This book has been tried and tested in the classroom by hundreds of civil and military students from all over the world who have benefited from the concise, informative and practical writing style.

"Basic Gas Turbines for Helicopter Pilots" is written in plain English with easy-to-understand explanations supported by many photographs, illustrations and diagrams. It is a comprehensive text that is a must for the helicopter pilot exploring the world of turbine engines.

About the Author

Mike Becker is one of Australia's most experienced helicopter instructors, with over 16,000 hours of rotary-wing flight experience. His career has taken him from the mountains in New Zealand to the outback of Australia, to the jungles of Papua New Guinea. He has also worked in the United States, Italy and Borneo.

He has flown a range of helicopter types – the Robinson R22, Robinson R44, Bell 47, Hughes 269, Hughes 500, Bell 206, Bell 427, Bell 212, EC120, Dragon Fly, Brantley B23, Enstrom EF28, Sikorsky S62A, Hiller

H12ET, Aerospatial AS350, Agusta 109E Power, Agusta 109S Grand, and the Agusta 119 Koala.

He is experienced in a vast range of helicopter operations including high altitude, remote area operations, mustering, firefighting, tourism, sling load operations, specialised longline operations, search and rescue, and Night Vision Goggles operations.

Mike is a Grade One Flight Instructor and Flight Examiner who holds an Australian Air Transport Pilots Licence (Helicopter) and an Australian Commercial Pilots Licence (Fixed Wing).

Mike is the Chief Pilot and Head of Training for his own business Becker Helicopters in Australia. He, and his wife Jan, established Becker Helicopters in 1997 with one Bell 47 and have grown the business through a love of helicopters, hard work, and determination.

Mike is the recipient of many awards, including the "Captain John Ashton Award for Flight Standards and Aviation Safety" by the Guild of Air Pilots and Air Navigators of London, which was awarded in recognition of over 18,000 accident-free flight training hours at Becker Helicopters. Mike has also authored "Mike Becker's Helicopter Handbook", first published in 1986, along with a range of theory books and instructional videos.

Mike Becker, Becker Helicopters

Brief History

Hero of Alexandria, an Egyptian mathematician and philosopher in the first century AD, demonstrated the earliest known "Reaction" or "Jet" engine. This experimental steam-operated device (or toy) was called the AEOLIPILE and although it had no practical use, it did demonstrate that a jet of steam escaping from the rear of a cauldron of boiling water will propel it forward. It worked by the cauldron being filled with water and then being suspended over a fire. When the water boiled the steam was allowed to escape out of purposely bent pipes that would provide thrust and therefore try to turn the container about its supports (as shown in the diagram.)

In 1629, Italian engineer, Giovanni Branca, developed a steam turbine. His invention directed a jet of steam against a turbine wheel, which in turn powered a stamp mill.

This mechanism is actually on display in the British Museum and is said to be the forerunner of modern turbo-superchargers used on reciprocating engines.

In the early 1930s, several patents were awarded to European engineers working on gas turbine engines, but it is generally accepted that the British aeronautical engineer, Sir Frank Whittle, designed the first practical form of the modern gas turbine engine.

With the advent of WWII, the turbo jet engine was developed rapidly to the turbine engines we see today.

[1]

Replacement of the Piston Engine by the Turbine Engine

The main requirements of an aircraft engine are that it should have the least possible size and weight for a given power output. For an internal combustion engine, these objectives are achieved by passing a large mass flow of air through the engine by use of high RPM and obtaining as much work as possible out of each pound of air by using high maximum pressures and temperatures.

The main reason for the advent of the turbine engine over the piston engine is the high power/weight ratio because it can operate at higher RPM than the piston engine by virtue of its purely rotary motion. The RPM of the piston is limited by the heavy loads caused by reciprocating (change of direction as in up/down piston) and the effect of the piston/cylinder friction on horsepower lost.

Basic Gas Turbines *for Helicopter Pilots*

A great illustration of the comparison between piston and turbine can be made with one of the largest piston engines ever built, the R-4360, a 28-cylinder radial engine commonly called the "corncob" that was capable of supplying 4000 horsepower, and the JT9D turbine engine which powers the Boeing 747. The 747 would need 23 of the radial engines to do the same job that the four turbine engines are doing!

Figure 1 Largest piston engine ever built

Figure 2 JT9D turbine engine which powers the Boeing 747

Other advantages of the turbine versus the piston are:

- The development time for a turbine is approx. a quarter the time required to design, build and bring to the point of operation a piston engine.
- Production time is also shorter for the turbine due to the reduced number of parts than in a comparable piston.
- In the turbine, power is continuously produced compared to the intermittent cycle of the piston. This will lead to relatively low working pressures and light construction of engine structure, ducting and casings. This is an important factor in power to weight calculations.
- Because there are only rotating parts and no reciprocating parts, turbine engine vibration is all but eliminated. This leads to a lighter airframe.
- The absence of reciprocating parts allows for higher operating speeds to be used. This leads to smaller space requirements and front area. The power to weight ratio is improved and significant weight savings are made. In fact, the turbine is about a quarter the weight of a comparable piston.
- A turbine will operate more efficiently at high altitudes; therefore, no turbo or supercharging system is required to maintain performance.

In summary, the turbine engine is simpler, requires less maintenance, has longer overhaul life, and offers greater reliability.

Mike Becker, Becker Helicopters

Basic Jet Propulsion Principles

Reaction principle

Jet propulsion is defined as the reacting force produced by the acceleration of air, gas, or liquid through a nozzle. However, it is not the air, gas or liquid being fired out the back that is producing the thrust (even though in an atmosphere it does help) but it is the internal pressure pushing the object forward.

To understand this we can use the example of a balloon. When a balloon is inflated, the inside air pressure which is stretching the skin is greater than the outside pressure. With the stem of the balloon tied closed, the inside air pressure pushes equally in all directions and the balloon will not move. (This is assuming it does not get blown by the wind, pushed or otherwise influenced.)

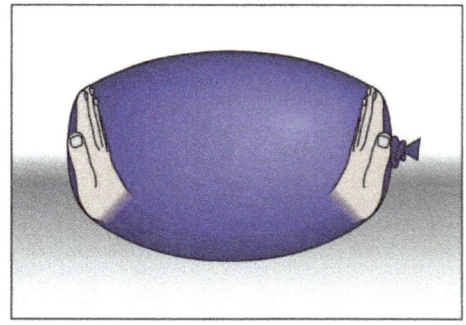
Figure 3 Equal pressure inside a balloon

If we now place the balloon in a vacuum (like in space) and then release the stem, the escaping air will have nothing to push against yet the balloon will still move in a direction away from the stem just as it does in a normal atmosphere.

This is because releasing the stem removes a section of the skin on that side of the balloon against which air has been pushing, however on the side directly opposite the stem the air continues to push, and it is the push on this area that causes the balloon to move in the direction away from the stem.

This is known as the "**Reaction Principle**" and it underlies all forms of jet propulsion. It is an example of Newtons Third law of physics which states "for every action, there is an equal and opposite reaction."

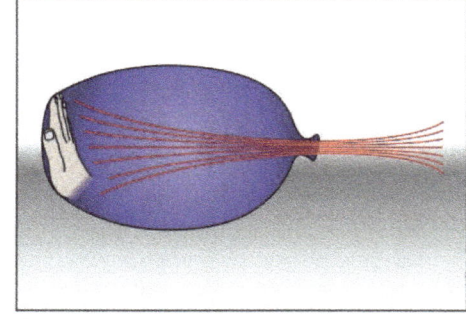
Figure 4 Unequal pressure inside the balloon moves the balloon

Summary

Jet propulsion comes not from the escaping air pushing against anything outside, but from the reaction force inside the engine (as in the balloon example).

Gas Laws

Since a turbine engine involves gases, it is appropriate, therefore, that we explain each of the Gas Laws as they explain the behaviour of air as it passes through a turbine.

The gas laws explain the relationship between the absolute temperature (T), pressure (P) and volume (V) of gases (air), they include:

- Charles' Law: relating to volume and temperature,
- Boyle's law: relating to pressure and volume,
- Gay-Lussac's Law: relating to pressure and temperature,
- Combined Gas Law.

Charles' Law

Charles' Law states that at constant pressure, the volume of a given mass of gas is directly proportional to its absolute temperature.

> **Formula**
>
> The formula for Charles' Law is as follows:
>
> **Volume (V) divided by Temperature (T) equals a constant (K)**
>
> $$V / T = K$$

Boyle's Law

Boyle's Law states that at a constant temperature, the pressure and the volume of a gas are inversely proportional.

> **Formula**
>
> The formula for Boyle's Law is as follows:
>
> **Pressure (P) times Volume (V) equals a constant (K)**
>
> $$P \times V = K$$

Gay–Lussac's Law

Gay-Lussac's Law states that at a constant volume, the pressure of a given mass of gas is directly proportional to its absolute temperature.

Simply put, if a gas's temperature increases then so does its pressure, if the mass and volume of the gas are held constant.

> **Formula**
>
> The formula for Gay-Lussac's Law is as follows:
>
> **Pressure (P) divided by Temperature (T) equals a constant**
>
> $$P / T = K$$

Combined Gas Law

The Combined Gas Law states that the ratio between the pressure-volume product and the temperature of a system remains constant.

The Combined Gas Law 'combines' Charles' Law, Boyle's Law and Guy-Lussac's Law.

These three laws each relate one thermodynamic variable to another while holding everything else a constant.

- Charles' Law states that volume and temperature are directly proportional to each other as long as pressure is held constant.
- Boyle's Law states that pressure and volume are inversely proportional to each other at a fixed temperature.
- Gay-Lussac's Law introduces a direct proportionality between temperature and pressure as long as it is at a constant volume.

Formula

The interdependence of these three laws and their variables is shown as follows:

Pressure (P) times Volume (V) divided by Temperature (T) equals a constant

$$P \times V / T = K$$

Summary

Jet engines are basically gas engines in that gas (air) is sucked in through an intake, squeezed, heated and pushed out through turbine wheels and exhaust tubes. . Various ducts, tubing and nozzles alter temperature, and pressure as the air travels through the engine, the result is energy that is harnessed to propel or drive something.

Types of Jet Engine

There are four common types of jet engine, they are the:

- Rocket Jet
- Ram-jet
- Pulse-jet
- Turbine Jet, including Turbofans, Turboprops and Turboshaft

Rocket Jet

The Rocket Jet is a non-air breathing engine, which simply means it does not use atmospheric air to support combustion but carries its own oxidizer and fuel. (In either solid or liquid form.)

Combustion transforms small volumes of this fuel into large volumes of gases. The gases released by combustion escape through an exhaust nozzle at extremely high velocity. The thrust reaction from the exhaust gases drives the rocket at very high supersonic speeds and completely out of the earth's atmosphere.

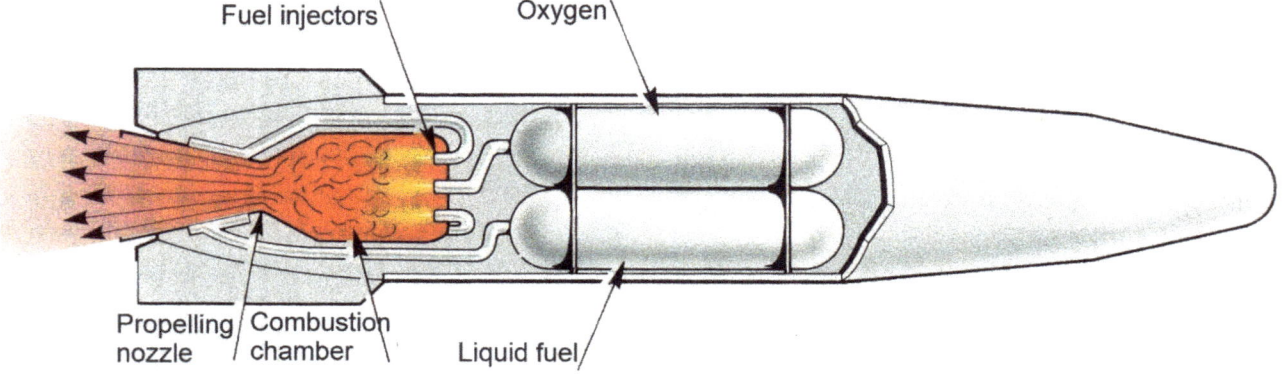

Ram-jet

The ram-jet or aero-thermodynamic duct (athodyd for short) is the simplest type of power plant with no moving parts that uses the atmosphere to support combustion.

It is a duct designed to receive inlet air and change its velocity into static pressure. Fuel is added to compressed air, with the resultant combustion and expansion of gases. The combustion causes the mass airflow to quickly exit the engine. The change in velocity of entering and departing air results in reactive thrust pushing the ram-jet forward as in our balloon example.

The disadvantage of a ram-jet is that it needs to be moving forward at a high speed before it can be started. It cannot function at low speed or at rest.

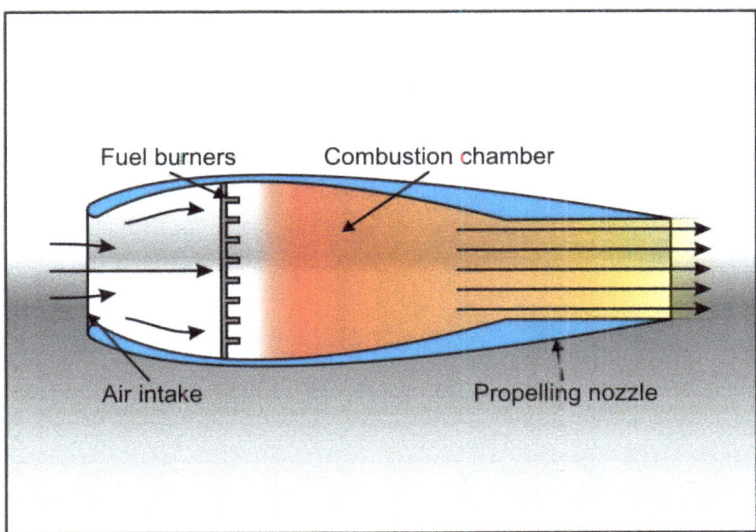

Pulse-jet

The pulse-jet is similar to the ram-jet except that the pulse-jet is fitted with a system of air inlet flapper valves. These valves are closed during combustion and provide the device with a moderate static thrust that the ram-jet does not have. This intermittent combustion cycle, caused by the flappers, causes a series of rapid backfires or pulses, which creates forward thrust.

A loud buzzing sound also results from the frequency of the cycle which may be repeated several thousand times a minute. (Have you ever heard of the Buzz Bomb? This was how it was powered.)

The pulse-jet, like the ram-jet, requires an airflow through the engine before it can start but once started it is self-sustaining.

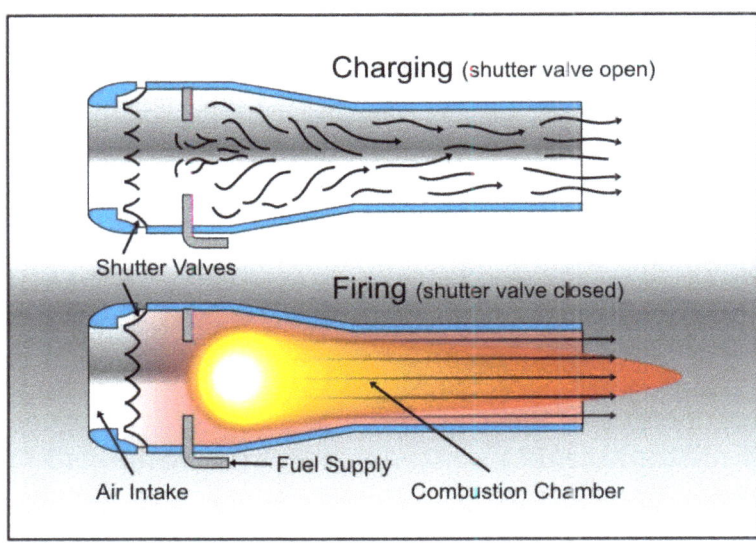

Both the pulse-jet and the ram-jet were used in propelling helicopter rotor blades with several of these engines built for this purpose. The engines themselves were built into the tip of the rotor blades taking away the torque reaction found in conventional helicopters.

The high tip speeds of the rotor blades are ideal for the ram-jet and the smoothness of the engine (particularly the ram-jet) is ideal for helicopters. Despite the high fuel consumption (approximately double that of a turbine engine) the saving in weight due to its simplicity and the absence of a drive shaft, torque and vibration has advantages in drastically reducing the structural weight. The greatest drawback is the large amount of noise it produces.

Figure 5 Little Henry, made by Hughes, powered by ram-jets on the rotor blade tips

Figure 6 Army XH-26 Pulse Jet Helicopter

Basic Gas Turbines *for Helicopter Pilots*

Turbine Jet

The most common form of jet power utilized today is that of the turbine or turbo jet.

(Commonly called the turbo jet because it is basically a jet with a turbine placed at the exhaust port to make use of the exiting gases. The turbine is attached to a shaft that drives a compressor, in effect turbo charging the jet engine).

The turbine jet has avoided many of the inherent weaknesses of the rocket and ram-jet by introducing a turbine wheel and a compressor as a means of producing thrust when stationary or at low speeds.

Unlike the rocket and the ram-jet the "turbine jet" engine operates on a working cycle as it draws air in from the atmosphere and after compressing and heating it, the energy and momentum given to the air is forced out at the propelling nozzle at a velocity up to 2000 feet per second or about 1400 miles per hour (2240 km per hour). On its way through the engine, the air gives up some of its energy and momentum to drive the turbine, which powers the compressor to keep the cycle going. This cycle is known as the Brayton Cycle.

Turbine jets come in various shapes, configurations and sizes depending on the manufacturer's requirements of power, weight, space available and use.

Typically they can be divided into three categories, Turbofans, Turboprops and Turboshafts.

Turbofans

The turbofan engine is similar to the turbo jet except it also employs extra turbine stages to drive a "fan" typically mounted at the front of the engine but also possible to be mounted at the rear of the engine. The fan accelerates air around the outside of the engine core and produces typically 75% of total thrust. It is more efficient because it moves larges masses of air at a slower speed, rather than the pure jet which moves small masses of air at high speeds.

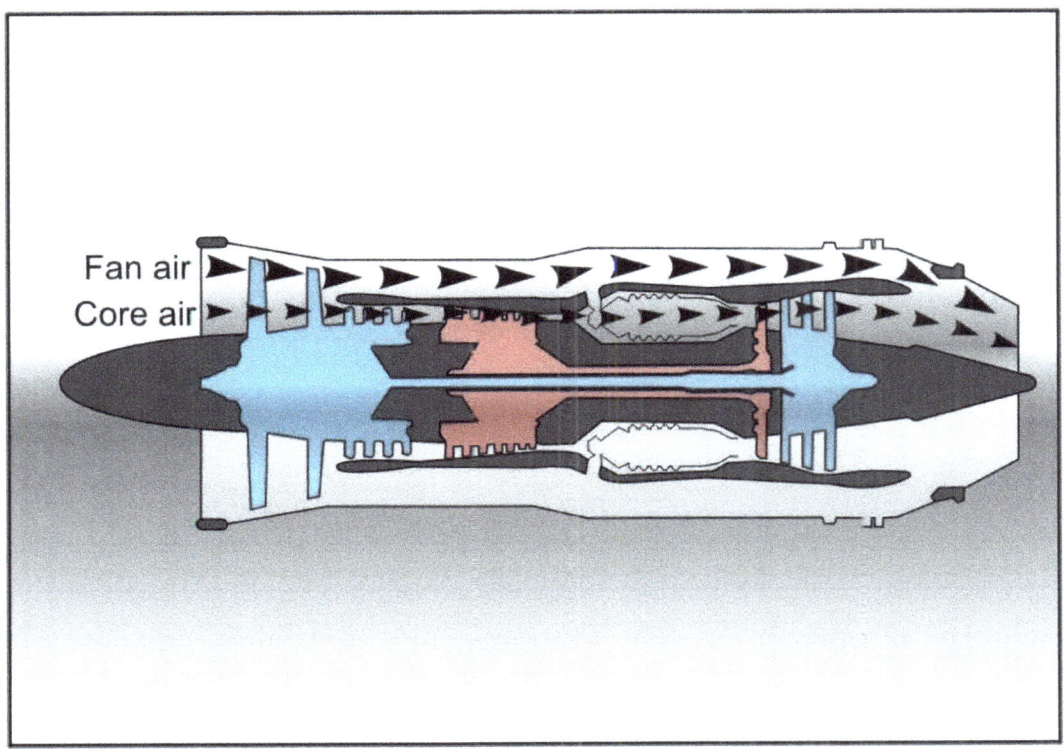

They were developed to provide a compromise between the best features of the turbo jet and the turbo prop in that with its ducted design the turbofan has turbo jet type cruise speed capabilities yet retains some of the short field take-off capabilities of the turbo prop.

For the same amount of thrust produced, the turbofan engine uses approximately 50% less fuel than the turbo jet and is much quieter because its exhaust velocity is slowed by the extra turbine stages.

Figure 7 Example of a turbofan engine[6]

Turbofan engines can be either High bypass or low bypass

Turbofan engines can be either high bypass or low bypass. This refers to the ratio of the amount of air that bypasses (or passes around) the core of the engine to the amount of air that passes through the core is called the bypass ratio. A low bypass engine does not bypass as much air around the core as a high bypass engine. On some front fan engines, the bypass stream is ducted overboard either directly behind the fan through short ducts or at the rear of the engine through longer ducts, thus the term "**Ducted Fan**".

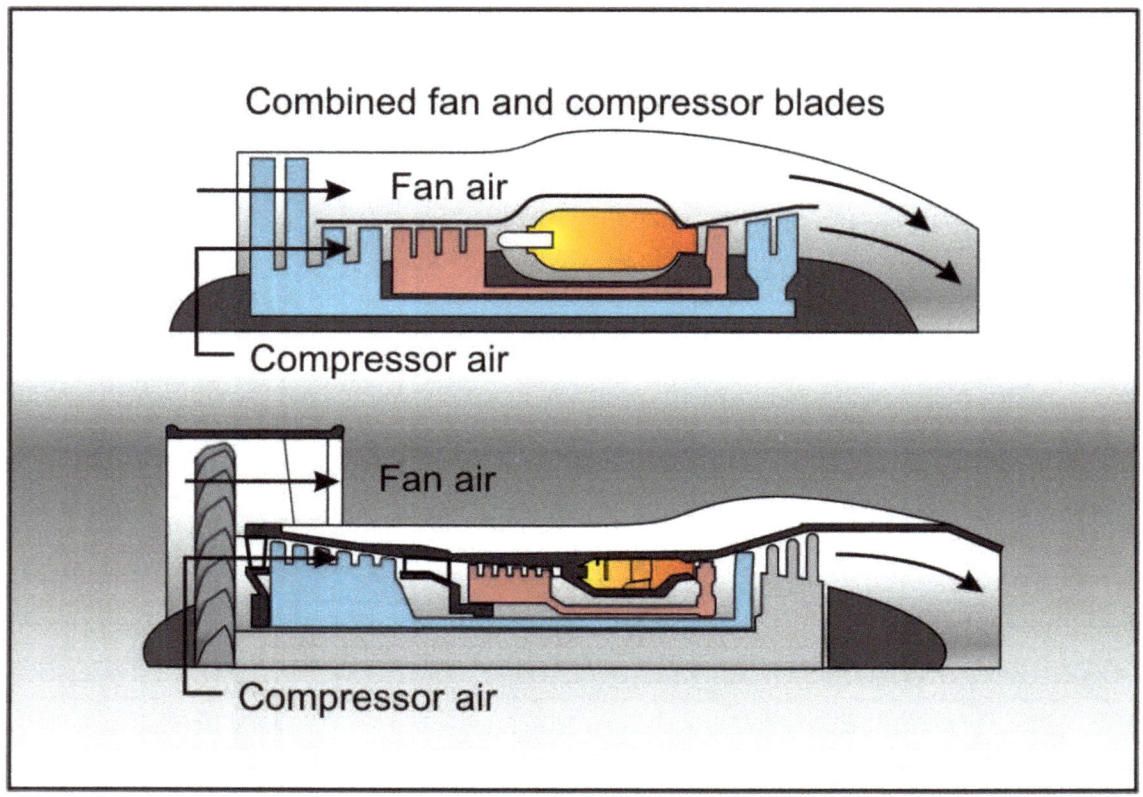

Basic Gas Turbines *for Helicopter Pilots*

High bypass

The high bypass engine utilizes a fan section of the compressor to bypass a large volume of air compared with the amount which passes through the engine core, usually around the 5:1 ratio or more (in other words 5 times the volume of air goes through the fan section compared to what goes through the compressor/turbine section).

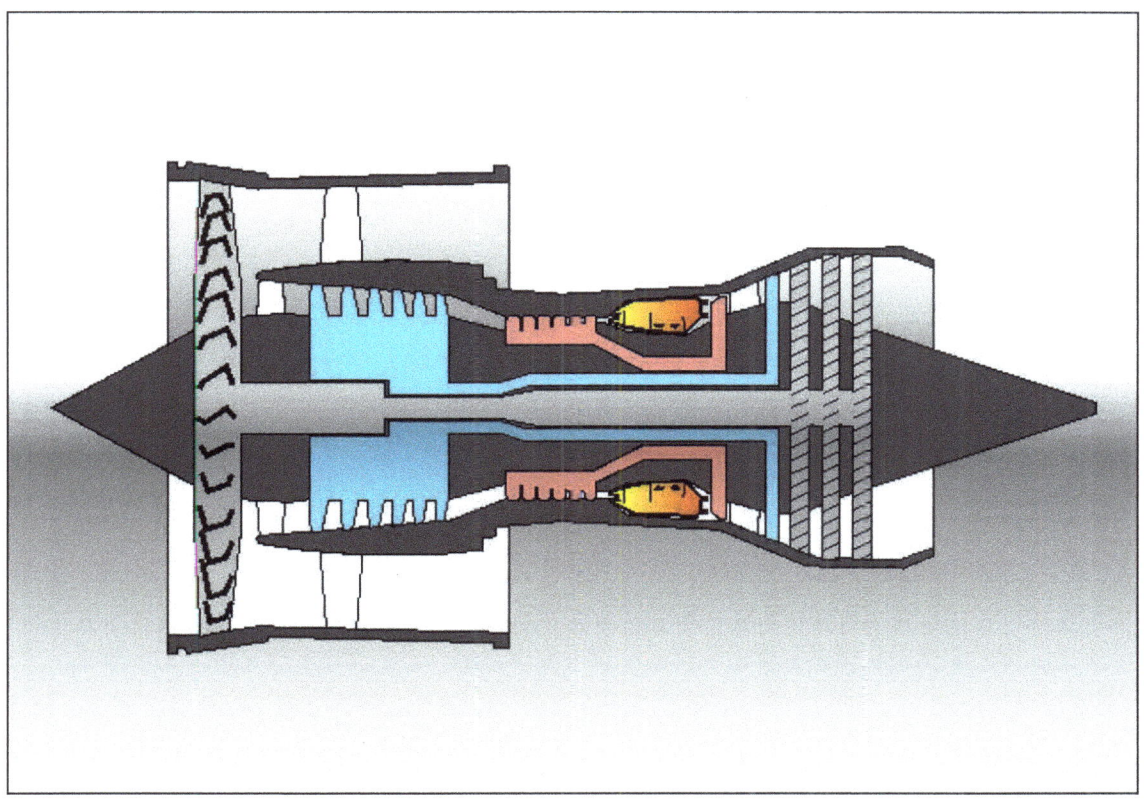

Low bypass

The Low bypass engine works in the same manner as a high bypass engine except it does not move as much air around the core. Normally the ratio is around 1:1.

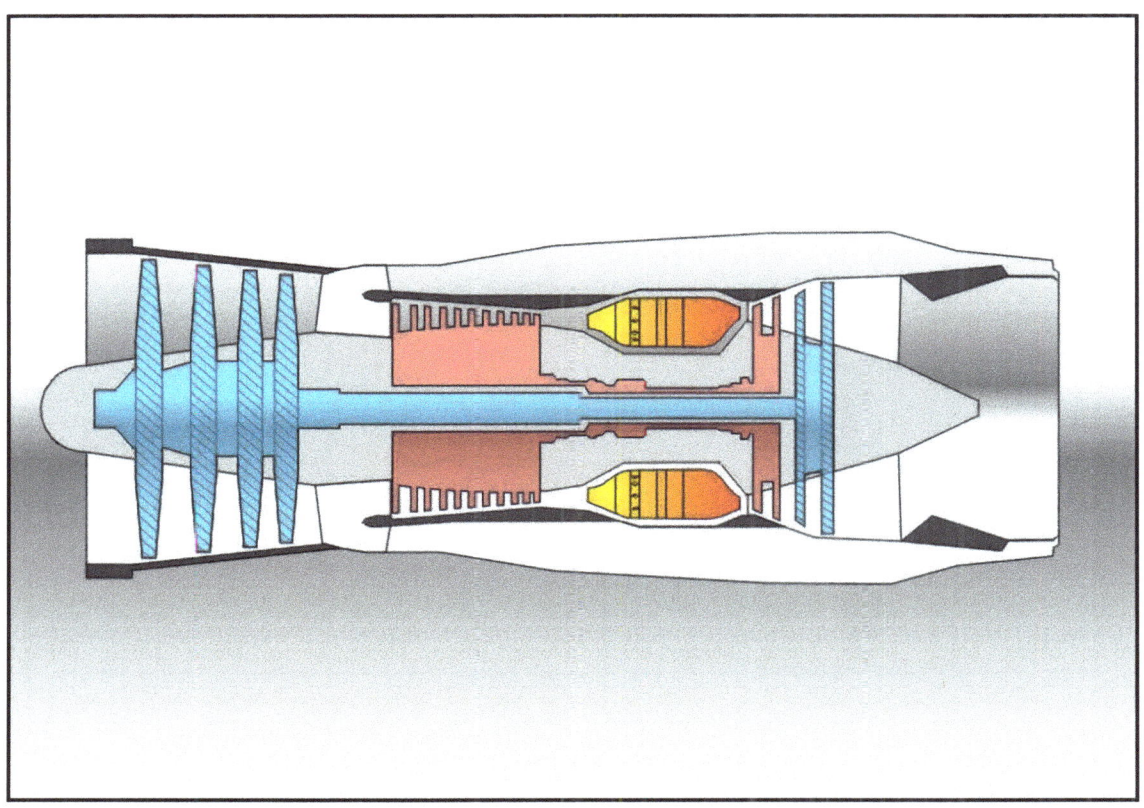

Mike Becker, Becker Helicopters

Low bypass with mixed exhaust

Low bypass with mixed exhaust moves air around the core as in the low bypass, but the air is then ducted to meet up with the exiting exhaust gases to come out the propelling nozzle as velocity.

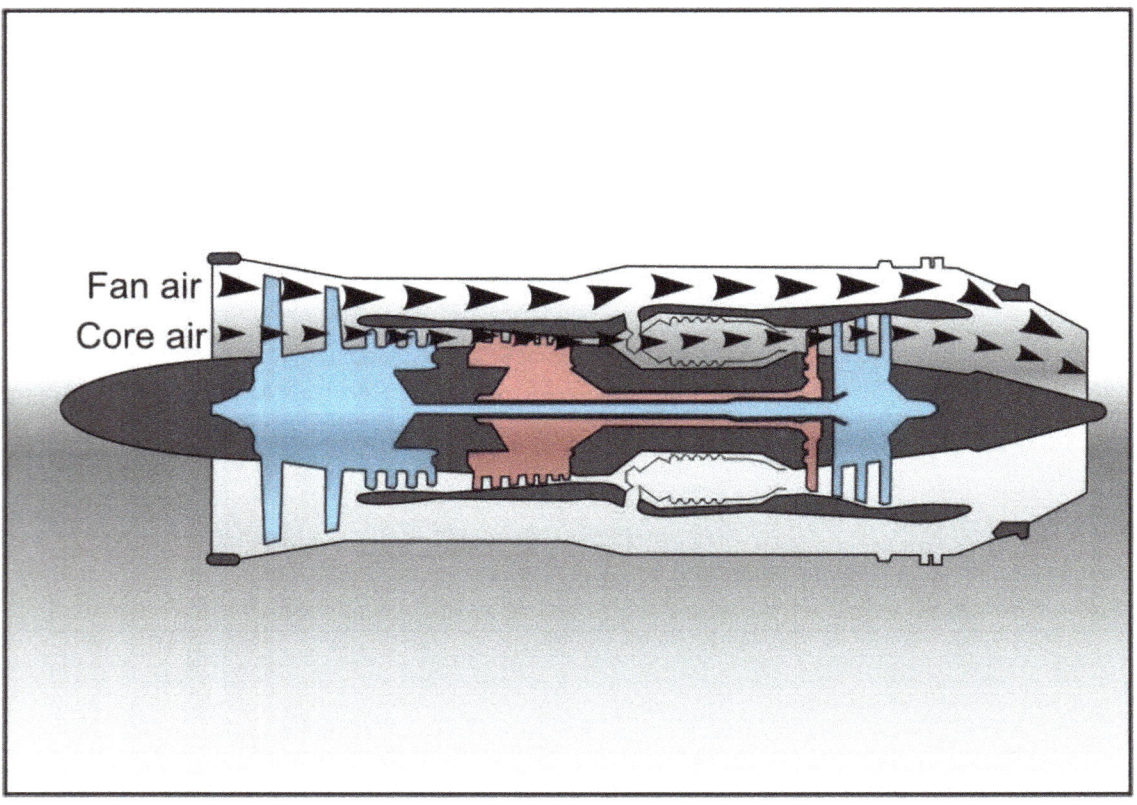

Rear fan and Prop fan

The rear fan and Prop fan has the fan at the rear of the engine and is an extension of the turbine. Recent developments in material construction have made these designs possible with a bypass ratio of 30 to 1 and even as high as 100 to 1. The big advantage of this design is the low fuel consumption.

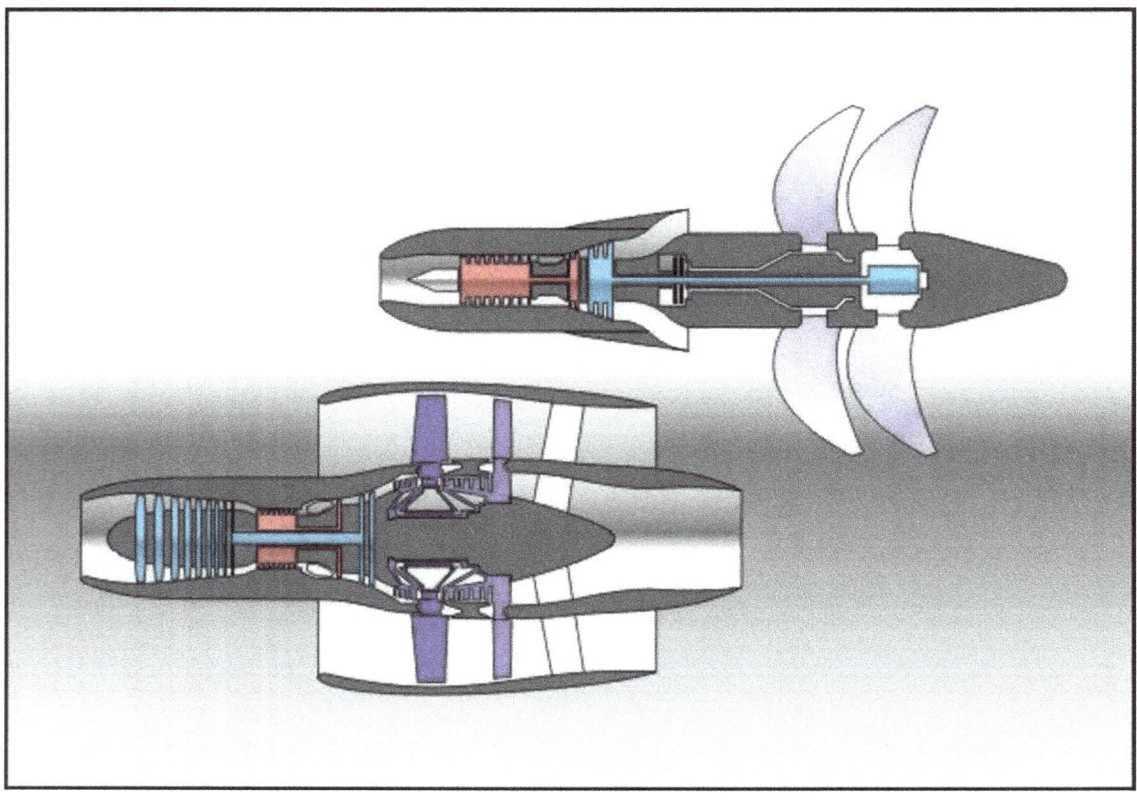

Turboprops

The turboprop engine is a gas turbine or turbo jet with a reduction gearbox mounted in the front or forward end to drive a standard aeroplane propeller.

These engines extract the energy of the jet exhaust by a turbine and use this energy to drive a gearbox. They do not rely on the thrust of the exhaust gases.

The turboprop will usually have more turbine stages, which are needed to drive the output reduction gearbox and the propeller. The total power of the turboprop is the sum of the propeller thrust and exhaust nozzle thrust (if there is any).

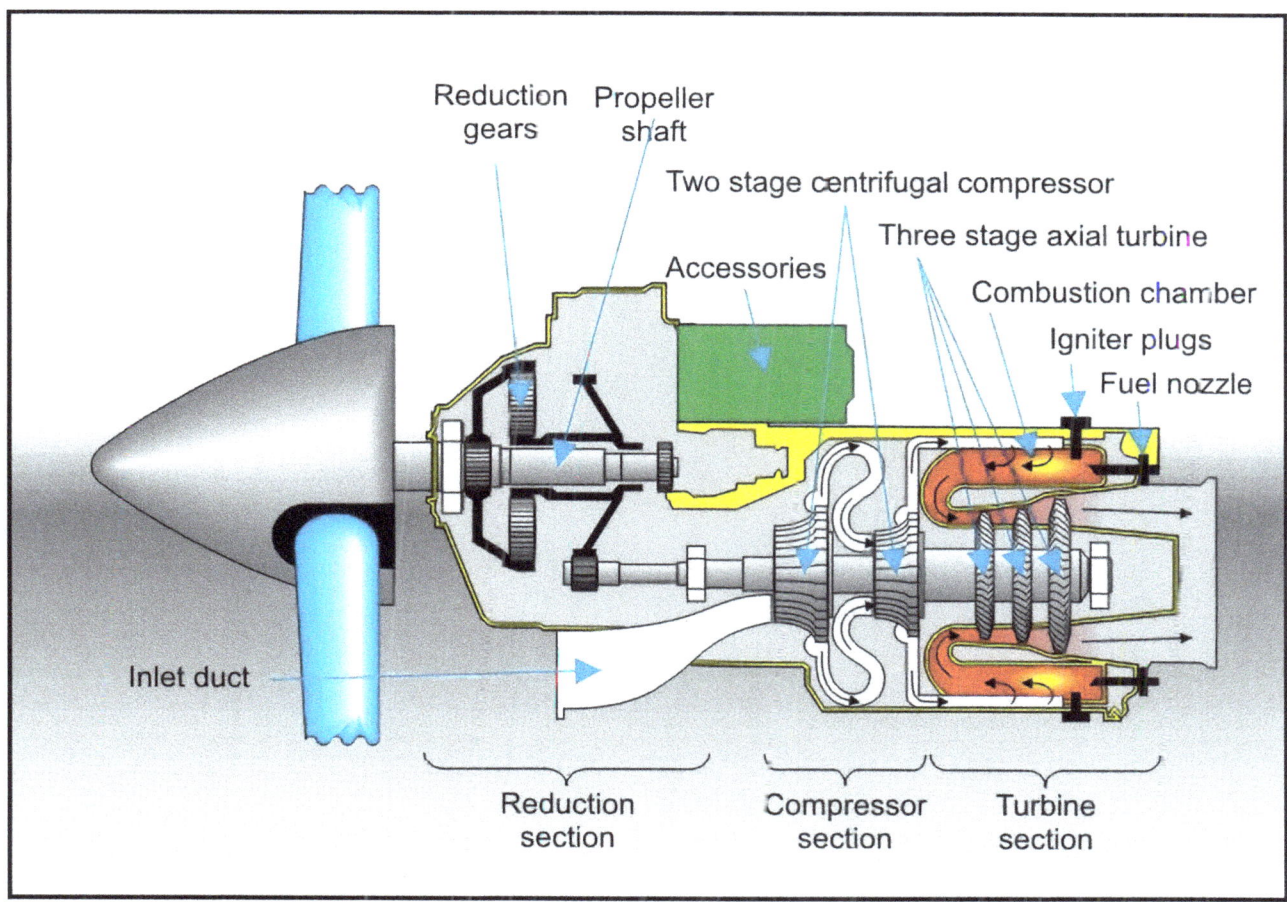

The propeller is driven by either a fixed or free turbine. The fixed turbine is connected directly to the compressor, reduction gearbox and propeller shaft. The free turbine is connected only to the gearbox and propeller shaft. This arrangement allows the free turbine to seek its optimum design speed while compressor speed is set at its design point of best compression.

Free power turbine schematic

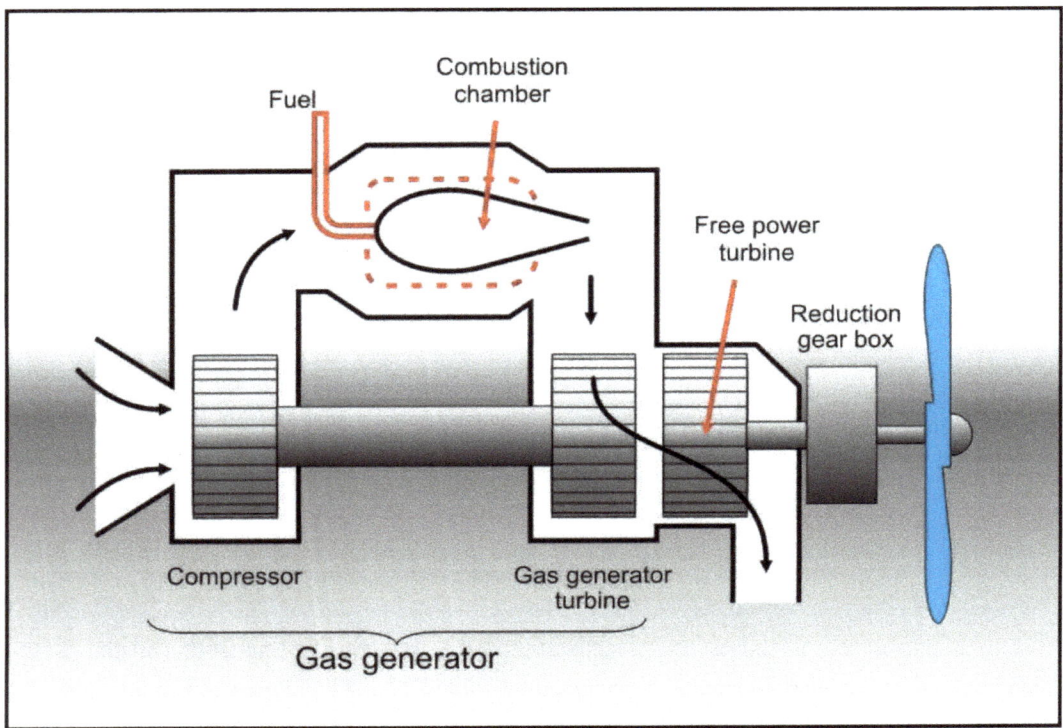

Fixed shaft power turbine schematic

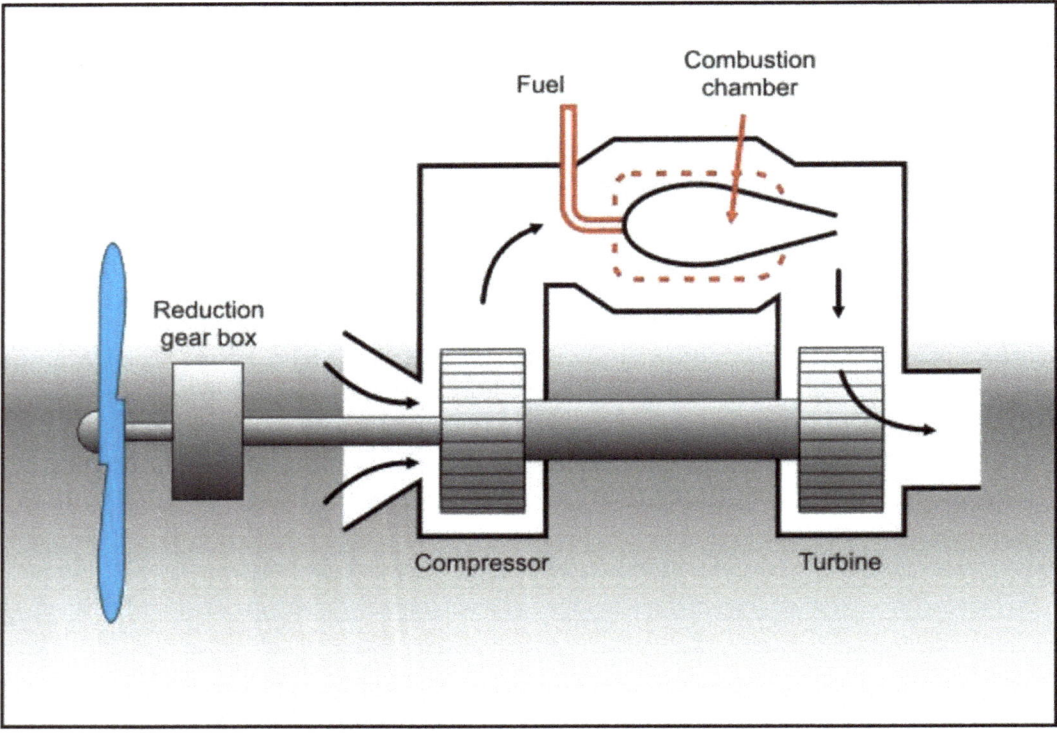

Some advantages of the free turbine are:

- The propeller can be held at very low RPM during taxiing with low noise and low blade erosion.
- The engine is easier to start, especially in cold weather.
- The propeller and its gearbox do not directly transmit vibrations into the gas generator.
- A brake can be used to stop the propeller during aircraft loading when an engine shutdown is not desired.

The main disadvantage is the engine does not have instantaneous power like that of reciprocating engines.

Turboshaft

A turboshaft's engine is a gas turbine engine that delivers power through a shaft to operate something other than a propeller (like a rotor system).

Many of the turbofan and turboprop engines are manufactured with minor variations into a turboshaft version. The turboshaft (or shaft turbine) may produce some thrust (but not necessarily) however its primary function is to produce shaft horsepower, (Shp) which in turn can be utilised to drive gearboxes and then rotor blades.

The power take-off may be coupled directly to the engine turbine or the shaft may be driven by a turbine of its own (free turbine as discussed previously).

Both types have been utilised to power helicopters, however, the free turbine is the most popular in use today.

[7]

Mike Becker, Becker Helicopters

How a Turbine Engine Works

An engine is defined as a machine or mechanical device for converting energy (usually supplied in the form of a chemical fuel) into motion or mechanical work.

As a helicopter pilot, the two engine types you will come into contact with are the piston and the turbine engine.

Both of these engines are classified as internal combustion engines because they obtain mechanical energy directly from the combustion of fuel burned in a combustion chamber that is an internal part of the engine.

In simple terms, in both engines air is taken in, compressed, fuel added and the mixture ignited, the resulting hot gas expands rapidly and is used to produce power.

We then harness this power to do work, in our case turn gearboxes and rotor blades etc.

The way the engines work are different

Piston engine

In a piston engine, all four "cycles" occur in one chamber, more commonly known as the "cylinder." Air is sucked into the chamber and then manipulated by the piston, spark plugs and valves so that every 4th cycle of the piston results in combustion. This combustion provides the force that moves the piston and thence the crankshaft to produce rotary or shaft power which is then transmitted through a gearbox to the rotor blades.

This means that in a piston engine, the burning of the fuel is **intermittent**: suck, squeeze, bang blow.

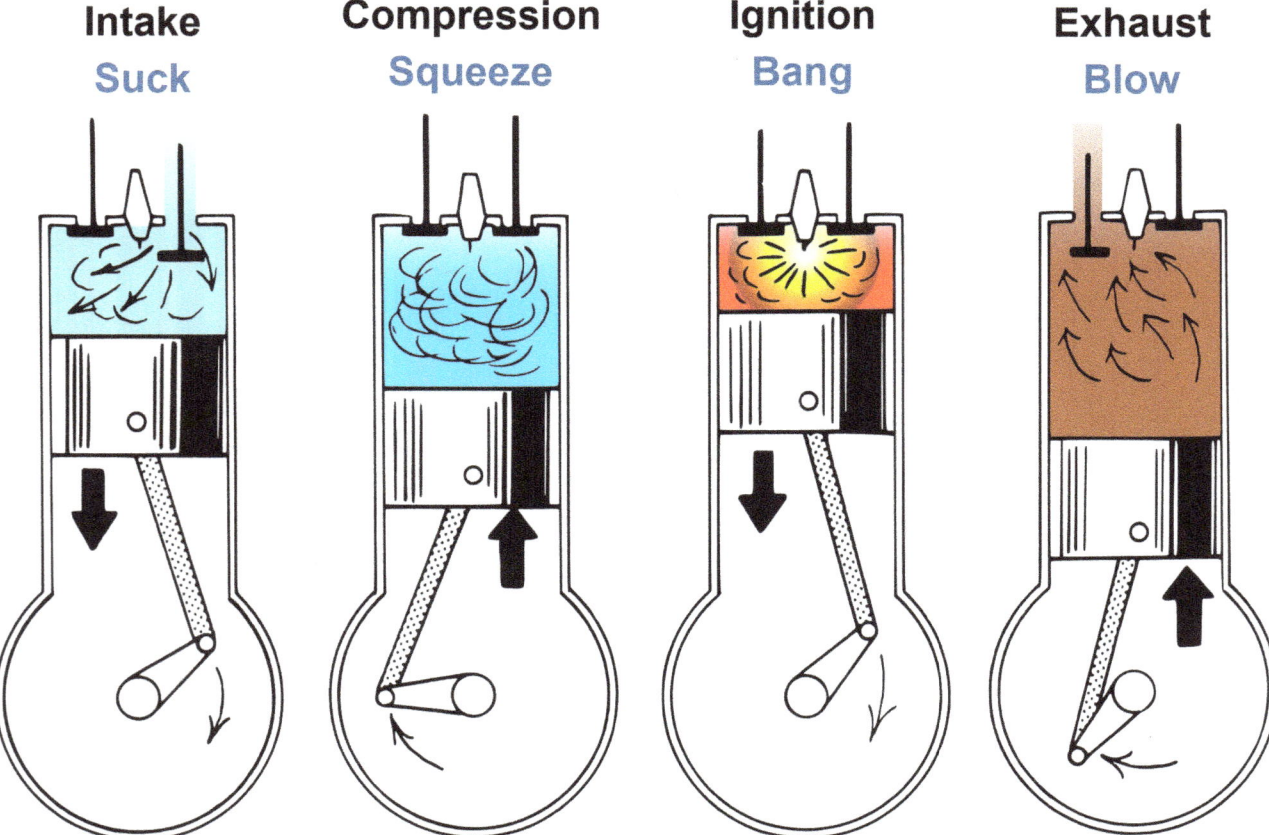

Basic Gas Turbines *for Helicopter Pilots*

Turbine engine

In a turbine engine, each of the four cycles occurs in a different section of the engine so the air moves in a continuous flow or "action" with a constant flame in the combustion chamber.

Once the turbine engine is started, the burning of the fuel is continuous and the expanding gas is ejected from the engine through the turbine wheels, which produces rotary or shaft power that is then transmitted through a gearbox to the rotor blades.

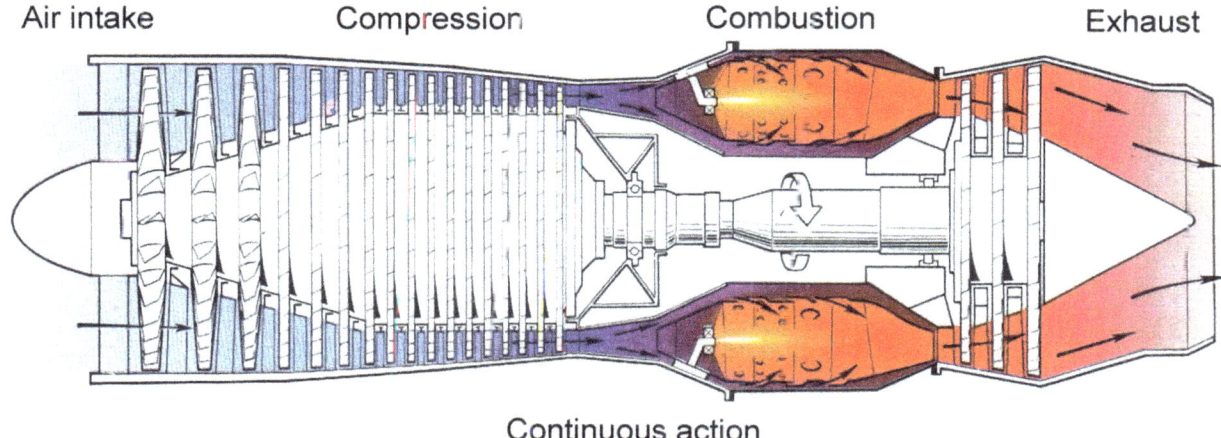

The Brayton Cycle

The continuous thermodynamic cycle of the gas turbine engine is known as the Brayton Cycle named after George Brayton, a Boston engineer, in the early 1900s. To understand this let's go back to our balloon example.

Let's assume that we have again released the stem of the balloon and we have an internal force with the air being propelled out the back.

If we now place a turbine wheel in the stem of the balloon it would be turned by the escaping air and in turn, could drive a shaft that could be connected to a propeller or gearbox and thence rotor blades etc.

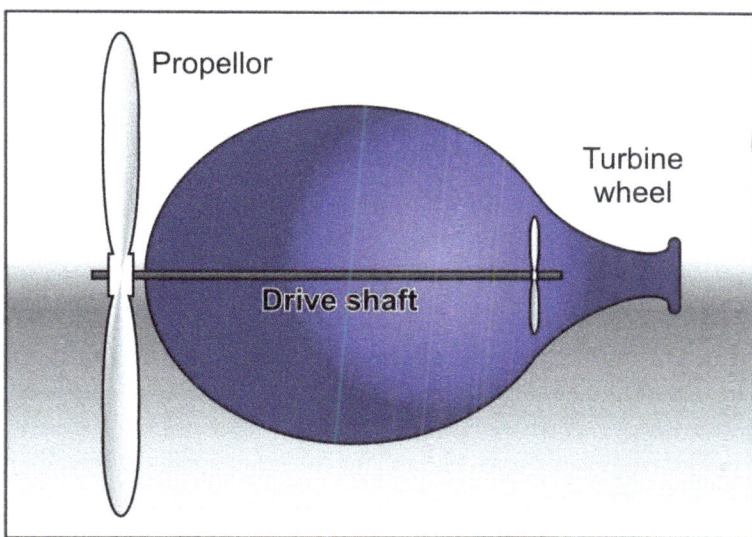

However, it is easy to see that the turbine wheel would stop turning once the pressure in the balloon has equalled the outside air pressure and there is no more movement of air exiting out the stem.

If we now open up the front of the balloon and used the turbine, through a series of fans to suck air in and compress it (make a simple compressor) we would again have our pressure differential and the turbine would continue to turn.

To complete the cycle we add fuel, ignite it so that the fuel is converted to energy which will further expand and accelerate the air leaving the balloon and we now have a self-sustaining cycle or a "turbo jet" more commonly called the basic gas turbine.

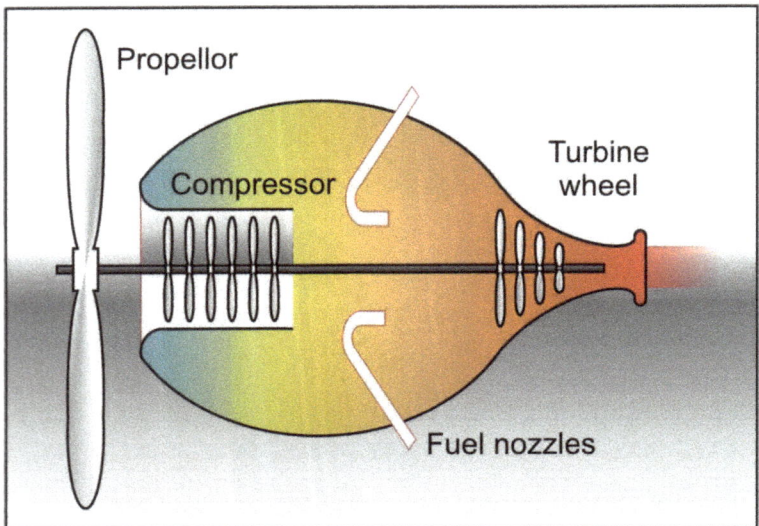

Of the useful energy leaving the combustion chamber, approximately 75% is extracted by the turbine. The remaining energy accelerates the gas as it passes through the propelling nozzle. A considerable amount of the energy available at the combustion chamber is not usable and is lost.

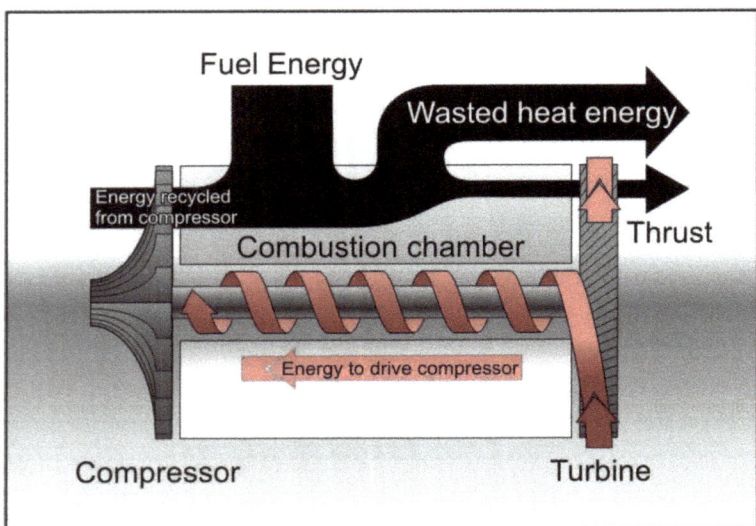

In both engine types, there is induction, compression, combustion and exhaust. In the case of the piston, these processes are intermittent with only one stroke being used to provide power. While in the gas turbine they occur continuously and so the three "idle strokes" are eliminated. This allows more fuel to be burnt in a shorter time, therefore, greater power output is achieved for a given engine size.

Due to the continuous action of the turbine engine and the fact that the combustion chamber is not an enclosed space, the pressure of the air does not rise during combustion but the volume does increase. The piston engine however will have an increasing pressure as the piston moves up the cylinder but it only has a constant volume to work with. A piston engine has peak pressures in excess of 1000 lbs/sq inch. This requires strong, heavy construction, and high-octane fuels, where the turbine need only use a light material in the combustion chamber and a low octane fuel.

It is important to remember, therefore, that in the gas turbine engine combustion occurs at **constant pressure with an increasing volume**, whereas in the piston engine the combustion process occurs at a **constant volume with increasing pressure**.

Pressure, Volume, Velocity and Temperature

During the working cycle of a basic gas turbine engine, the gas flow will take in and give out heat to produce changes in pressure, volume and temperature of the air mass. As changes occur, they are interrelated to conform to a combination of Boyles and Charles Laws. In other words, the product of the pressure and volume of an air mass is proportional to the absolute temperature of the air at that stage of its passage through the engine.

Raising the temperature of a gas will increase its volume (Charles Law). Where the gas flow is continuous and takes place within the confined limits of a turbine engine this change in volume is seen as a change in gas flow velocity. In other words, if there is a change in gas flow velocity there will be a change in the gas volume, therefore in a turbine when we talk about a change in volume, this is brought about by manipulating the velocity of the air flow.

Changes to the pressure, volume (velocity) and temperature of the gas flow occur in three main engine areas (stages):

- compressor
- combustion chamber
- turbine section.

Heat is a form of energy, variations in the heat content of the gases is directly proportional to the work done on the gases or energy taken from the gases during their passage through the engine.

Gas temperature is increased by compression and combustion, gas temperature is decreased as heat is extracted from the gases by the turbine to produce work.

Pressure Changes

Air enters the intake to the compressor at low pressure. There is considerable suction at the intake as the compressor is drawing in large quantities of air. In humid conditions, this may form intake ice and helicopters often have an anti-ice or de-ice system that the pilot has to activate given certain operating parameters. Often there is a warning light on the annunciator panel to warn if there is an ice build-up. The ice build-up can be dangerous for two reasons:

- Ice may form and block off the intake and the engine may starve of air and stop.
- Ice may break off and enter the compressor, causing damage and possible failure.

As air enters the compressor, the air pressure will continue to increase as it passes through each successive compressor stage, with the rate of increase rising. The compressor pressure ratio is determined by design and engine speed (RPM).

The Rolls Royce (Allison) 250 C20R engine is a typical helicopter turbine engine, pulling an overall pressure ratio of 8.0:1, at an airflow of 4.0 lb/s (1.8 kg/s), with a power output of 450shp (336 kW).

As the gas leaves the compressor section a final rise in pressure is accomplished in the divergent section of the diffuser.

From the diffuser, the gas passes through the combustion section where there is a slight pressure drop. Combustion pressure must be less than compressor pressure at all engine speeds to maintain a smooth flow of gas from intake to exhaust. If this flow is disrupted, then a compressor stall and surge would be encountered.

There is a sharp drop in pressure as the gas is accelerated between the convergent ducts of the turbine nozzle guide vanes and the pressure continues to drop across each successive turbine stage (nozzle and turbine wheel). As the gases leave the exhaust nozzle the pressure continues to drop to ambient.

Volume (Velocity) Changes

The velocity of the airflow entering the compressor must be less than the speed of sound (subsonic). This is obviously not a problem in a helicopter; however, in fixed-wing aircraft, such as high-speed military jets, this is going to be a problem so intake design for them is very important, but not worth discussing here.

Air flow velocity (and therefore volume) rises and falls marginally through each successive stage of an axial flow compressor and is considered to be constant overall. As the gas leaves the compressor velocity decreases through the diverging passage of the diffuser, then increases as the gas is forced into the inlet holes at the front and along the sides of the combustion chamber.

Once through the combustion process, velocity will increase sharply, this is accompanied by a corresponding decrease in pressure as the gas passes through the converging ducts of the turbine entry nozzle guide vanes. This exchange of pressure for velocity is required since the turbine is designed to convert high energy gases to aerodynamic forces to rotate the turbine wheels. A large portion of this energy (approximately 75%) is then absorbed by the first turbine wheel through a shaft to drive the compressor and engine accessories. The remaining energy (approximately 25%) is then absorbed by the remaining turbine wheels, through another shaft to drive the main transmissions and main and tail rotor blades.

Temperature Changes

Air enters the compressor at ambient temperature. This could be anywhere between -45°C to +60°C depending on where the helicopter is operating. (Arctic areas or hot desert areas.) As the air enters the compressor it is gradually warmed through each successive stage of the compressor leaving the compressor at approximately 300°C. As the gas now enters the combustion chamber and fuel is added and burned, combustion occurs, and the gas temperature rises as high as 1300°C across the whole combustion chamber. At the actual flame front, the temperature may be as high as 2300°C. Obviously, the metals that make up the combustion chamber and the turbine nozzles and wheels cannot handle that amount of heat without melting or being damaged therefore a large portion of the air coming from the compressor (approximately 75%) is used as a film of cooling air protecting the metal surfaces.

A turbine engine is a heat engine, therefore, the higher the gas temperature the greater the expansion of the gases and the better the engine efficiency will be, so it is a compromise in design to get the maximum heat without exceeding the tolerances of the materials.

Below is an example of the temperature, pressure and velocity (volume) of the various engine sections in a Rolls Royce 250C20B turbine engine.

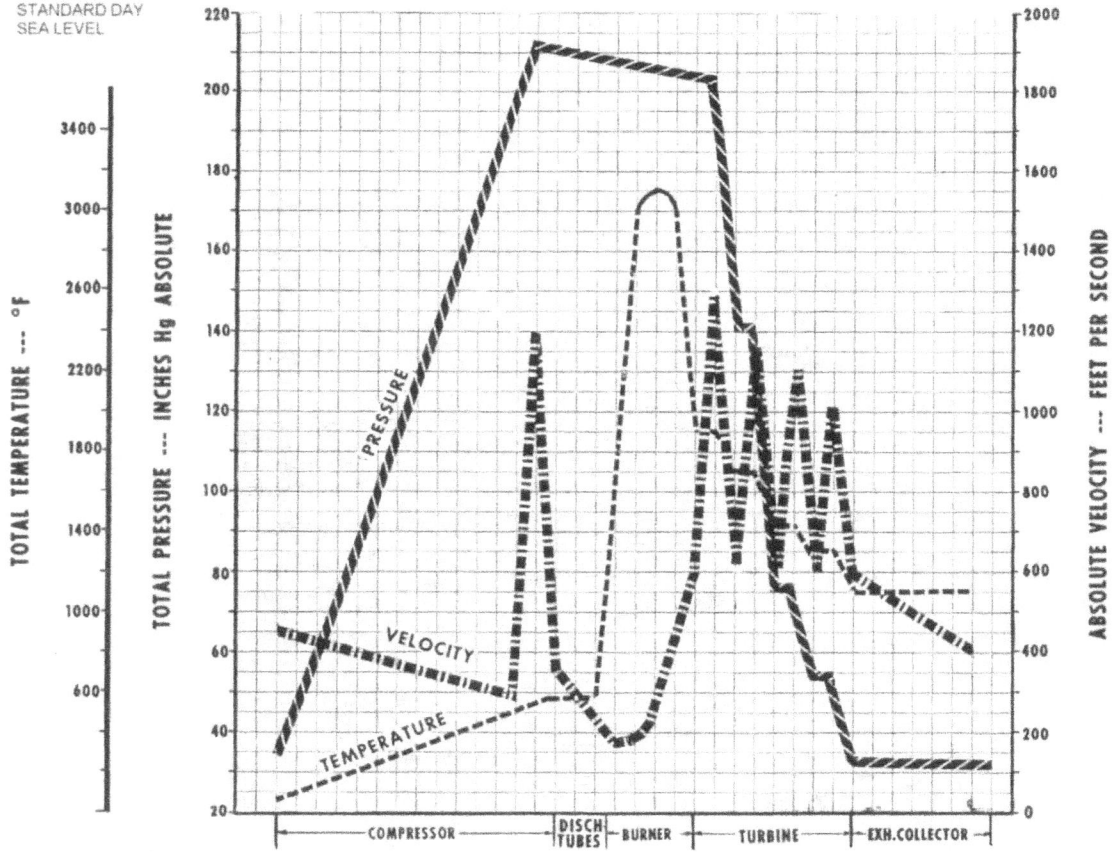

Ducting

To move air through a turbine engine and manage the varying and local requirements in each stage, a complicated and demanding design is required.

The shaping of passages, nozzles and wheels is very important. Internal turbulence leads to a loss of efficiency, eddies produce vibrations which can lead to component failure.

The gas turbine engine, therefore, uses varying types of divergent and convergent ducting to manipulate the airflow as required.

If the airflow is led through a convergent passage, the velocity must increase and there will be a drop in static pressure, density and temperature. This is the expansion process.

Conversely, a divergent passage causes a drop in velocity with a corresponding increase in pressure, density and temperature. This is the diffusion or compression process.

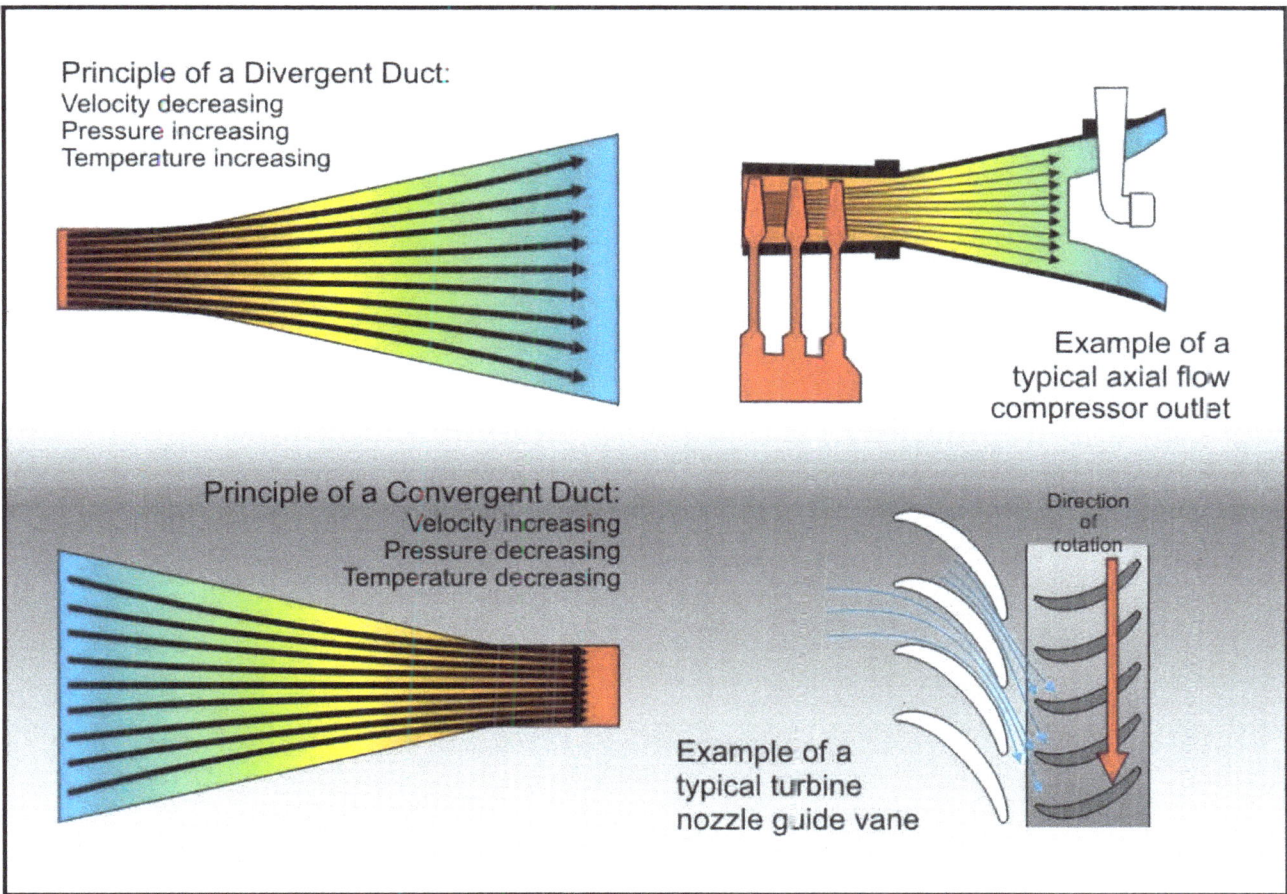

Summary

The path that a parcel of air takes through the engine will vary with design. A straight-through type will provide for an engine with a small frontal area, whereas a reverse flow type will have a larger frontal area and a shorter overall length.

With all types, the basic principles are the same.

Along its passage through the engine, aerodynamic and energy requirements demand changes in the pressure and velocity of the air.

Air Intake and Filters

The air intake and any associated filters are usually considered a part of the airframe and not of the engine. However, because the design of the intake and any aftermarket filters or particle separators that may be installed affect the flow of the air into the turbine engine, it is important that you have a working knowledge to best manage your engine.

Fixed Wing

Fixed-wing aircraft have their own set of problems. Unable to hover, they are designed to be moving forward at speed. The intake is therefore designed to straighten the air and if going at supersonic speeds (greater than the speed of sound) slow the air down at the intake.

Divergent ducts, Single and Double entrance intakes are designs that do this.

Some turbo prop aircraft (propellers) particularly those operating from bush strips will have a shrouded entrance. This is simply a crude particle separator of wire mesh fence that will prevent large obstacles such as stones or other foreign object debris (FOD0 from being drawn into the compressor.

Helicopters

Helicopter intakes are very simple, mainly because they operate at low speeds, often at the hover, so the turbine installation is designed not around the use of ram air (which is an advantage when moving forward) but around the worst-case scenario of maximum power at the hover with the wind coming from behind (tail wind hover).

Helicopters can have a range of filters installed at the intake or not have any filters at all.

Obviously, any filter will hinder the clean flow of air into the compressor and, therefore, a rise in temperatures can be expected. However, the added benefit of engine protection, overhaul life, and ultimately engine reliability far outweigh the loss of power that may be evident once the filter is fitted.

Intake Design

Intakes are designed to streamline the flow of air into the compressor so that the airflow arriving at the compressor face has an even pressure spread across the whole intake area without turbulent flow. Because a turbine engine draws in large quantities of air, any inefficiency in the intake duct will lead to a reduction in mass airflow and consequently a reduction in power output.

Air intakes in helicopters are usually located up high and are shielded, often with some form of an aerofoil in the middle to act as a guide vane to aid in the straightening of the air.

Often shielded, as helicopters have a habit of moving sideways, backwards, or hover in high crosswinds, the shielding allows the air to be drawn in and straightened regardless of the type of operation.

Jet Ranger intake

Agusta 109 intake

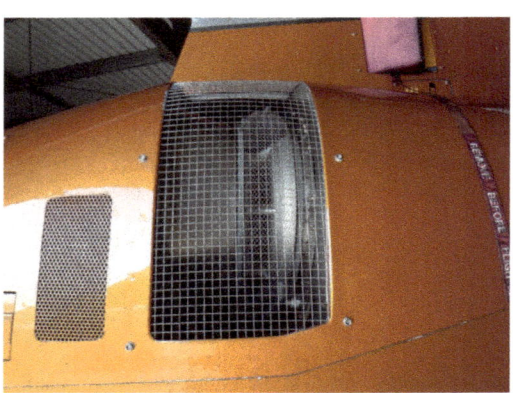

Intake Ice

As the compressor draws in air, it can form a local drop in pressure at the entrance to the compressor. Under certain ambient conditions, such as during forecast icing conditions or local areas of high humidity and low temperatures and operations around thunderstorms etc, this drop in pressure leads to a drop in temperature which can lead to ice forming on the intake.

Ice is obviously bad as it can:

- Form to such an extent that it blocks the intake and starves the engine of air causing a flameout.
- Break away from the intake and be ingested into the compressor, which can cause substantial damage and possible engine failure.

Indication of ice can be:

- If fitted with a warning light "INTAKE ICE".
- An increase in the turbine operating temperature for the same TQ setting.
- Flight in known icing conditions.

If intake ice is detected or suspected, then:

- Turn on the anti-ice system if fitted.
- Fly away from the affected area (if near a thunderstorm).
- Land as soon as possible and wait for conditions to improve.

Intake Filters

Particle separators, inlet barrier filters, sand filters, fine wire gauze filters are all names and differing designs for intake filters.

Because helicopters typically operate low to the ground in dirty environments stirring up dust, dirt, smoke, sea salt and other foreign objects, to best protect the engine from FOD (foreign object debris), operators and manufacturers install intake filters.

It is important that your filter is regularly serviced and kept clean. If a filter becomes blocked there will either be a manual or an automatic bypass system.

The disadvantage with filters is they act as a barrier restricting air flow into the compressor, this may increase turbine temperatures. The advantages, however, are protection for the compressor. The advantages far out weight the disadvantages.

Particle Separator

A particle separator uses small swirl vanes to rotate the air. Centrifugal force will then take out small particles of dirt by throwing them outwards to be collected in a tube and released overboard before the now clean air enters the compressor.

A particle separator is only good for larger particles is very easy to clean and does not require much maintenance. It does not usually have a bypass or pending blockage warning system as it is self-cleaning.

It is deemed to be a coarse filter in that it gives added protection to the compressor but is not as good as a purpose-built filter.

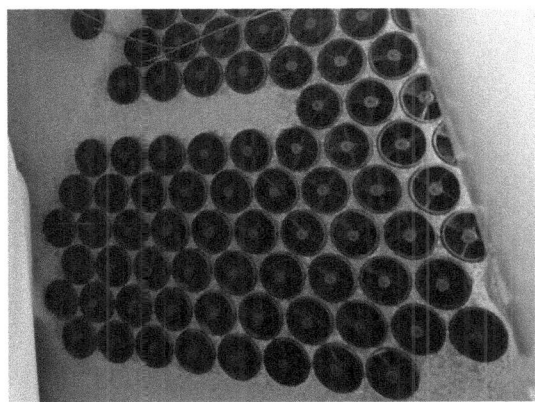

Figure 8 Particle separator in a Jet Ranger

Inlet Barrier Filter (IBF)

An inlet barrier filter may consist of fine wire micro mesh and a coating of oil, sand or paper filter. These filters take out even the smallest particles of dirt, dust, smog, smoke etc. and are considered to be very good pieces of equipment. They require frequent cleaning and maintenance to prevent clogging up and will come with a bypass and pending blockage warning system.

The IBF is a fine filter that gives added protection to the compressor extending its life and reducing overhaul costs.

Figure 9 IBF in a Jet Ranger

Basic Gas Turbines *for Helicopter Pilots*

Compressor Section

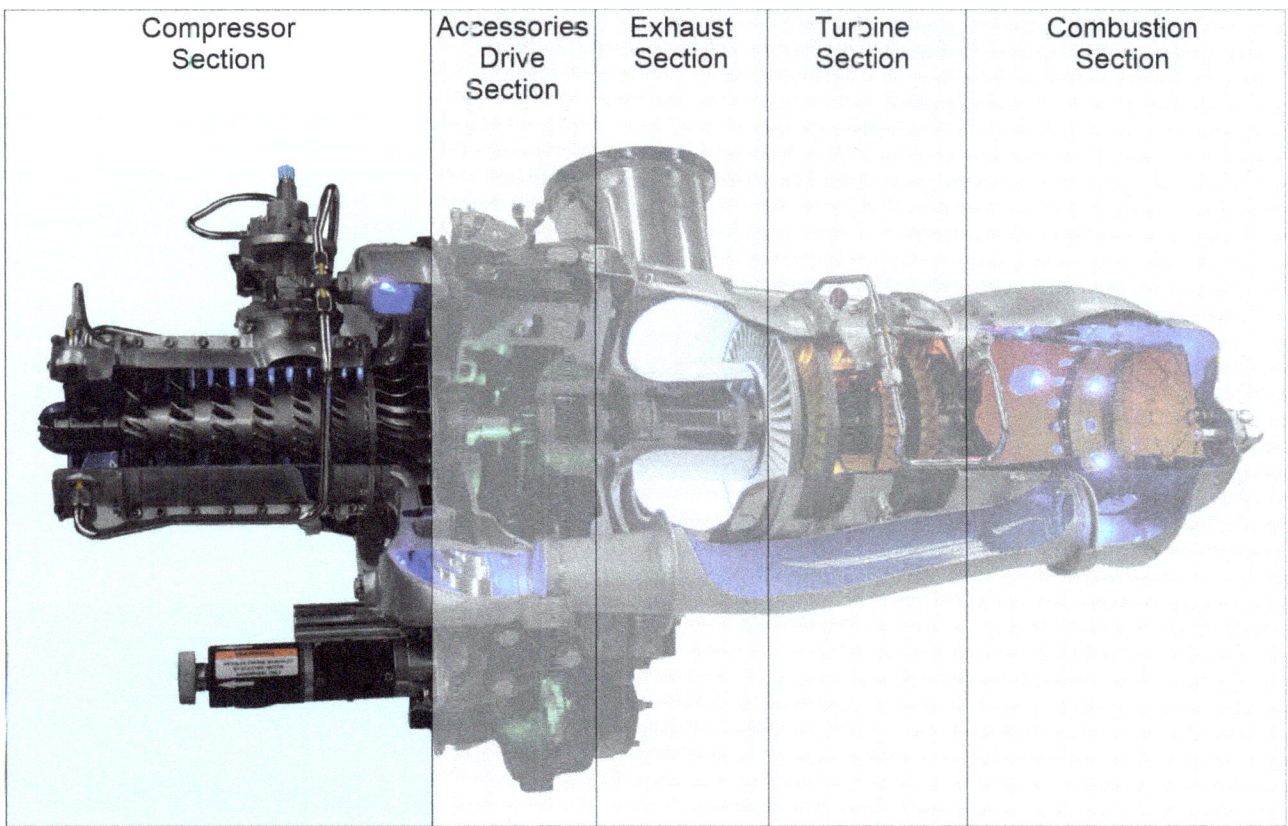

The combustion of fuel and air at normal atmospheric pressure will not produce enough energy to enable sufficient power to be extracted from the expanding gases to do a useful amount of work.

In both the reciprocating and the gas turbine engine, the fuel/air mixture must be compressed so that the maximum amount of air can be processed in a given volume.

Placed at the front of the engine, the compressor draws air in, pressurises it, and then delivers it into the combustion chamber via piping, or ducting called transfer tubes. There are two types of compressor design:

- Centrifugal flow (meaning a radial or outwards flow) compressor, and
- Axial flow (meaning straight through or inline) compressor.

Both types are driven by the engine N1 or Gas Producer turbine and are usually coupled directly to the N1 turbine by a shaft. Typically, both are 80% - 90% efficient. The connecting shaft goes through the accessories gearbox so can be turned over by the starter motor.

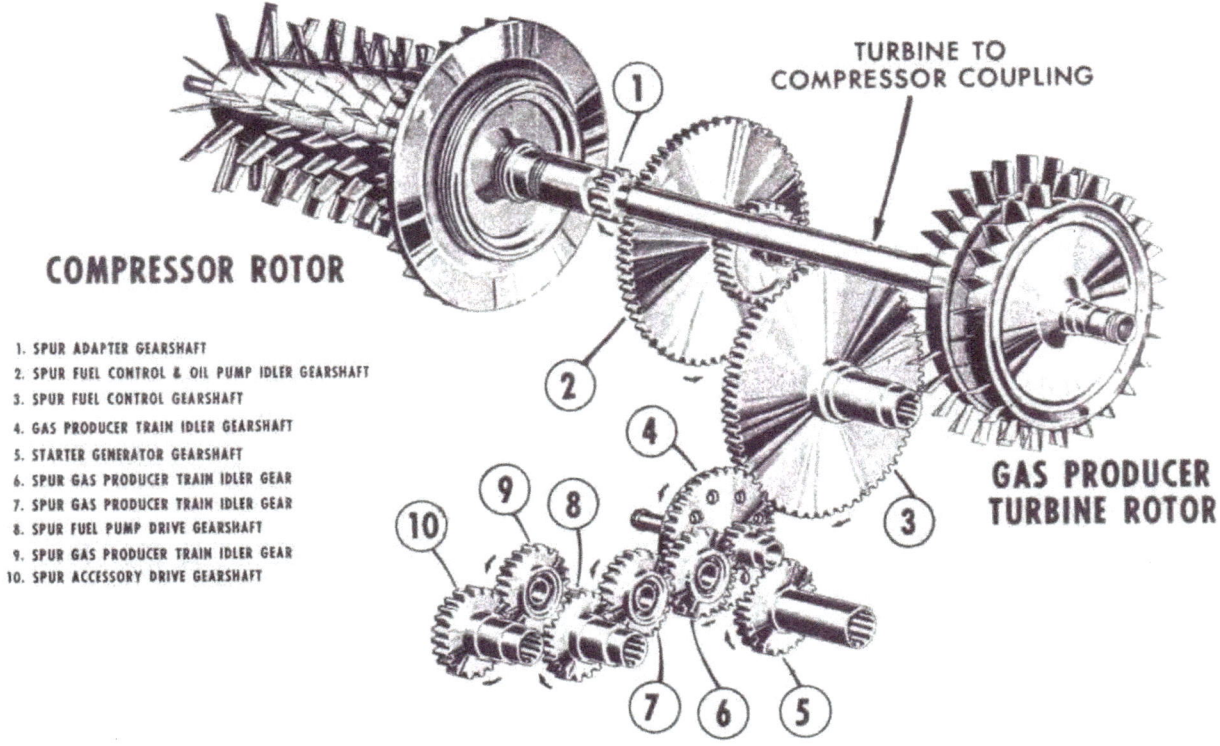

1. SPUR ADAPTER GEARSHAFT
2. SPUR FUEL CONTROL & OIL PUMP IDLER GEARSHAFT
3. SPUR FUEL CONTROL GEARSHAFT
4. GAS PRODUCER TRAIN IDLER GEARSHAFT
5. STARTER GENERATOR GEARSHAFT
6. SPUR GAS PRODUCER TRAIN IDLER GEAR
7. SPUR GAS PRODUCER TRAIN IDLER GEAR
8. SPUR FUEL PUMP DRIVE GEARSHAFT
9. SPUR GAS PRODUCER TRAIN IDLER GEAR
10. SPUR ACCESSORY DRIVE GEARSHAFT

The centrifugal compressor is more robust than the axial because there are fewer vanes and stators, which also makes the centrifugal compressor easier and cheaper to develop, manufacture and maintain.

An advantage of the Axial compressor is that it consumes much more air than a centrifugal compressor of the same frontal area and therefore, can be designed to achieve much higher compression ratios.

Even though an Axial flow compressor is more efficient than a centrifugal flow compressor, centrifugal compressors are favoured for small engines because of their rugged design and simplicity.

In some cases, such as the Allison 250 series engine, the two types are used together with the axial section of the compressor boosting the inlet pressure to the centrifugal section of the compressor.

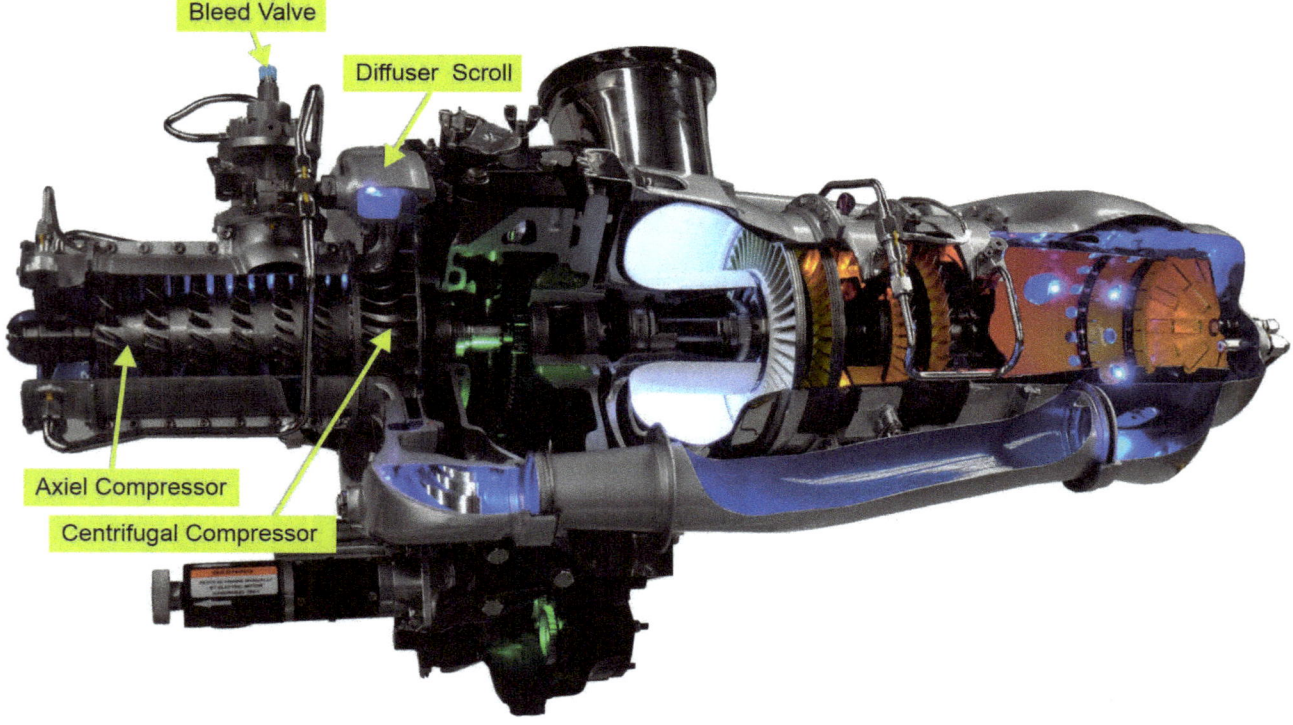

Pressure Ratio

The proportional increase in pressure through each stage of the compressor is called the compressor's pressure ratio. The compressor pressure ratio is determined by design and engine speed (RPM). A high-pressure ratio is the prime requirement of any compressor design.

The Rolls Royce (Allison) 250 C20R engine is a typical helicopter turbine engine, pulling an overall pressure ratio of 8.0:1, at an airflow of 4.0 lb/s (1.8 kg/s), with a power output of 450 SHp (336 kW).

The axial flow compressor can achieve a high degree of compressor efficiency within a range of pressure ratios whereas the centrifugal's compressor pressure efficiency peaks at a pressure ratio of about five then reduces dramatically.

A common feature of both centrifugal and axial flow compressors is that the specific fuel consumption of the engine decreases as the compression ratio rises and because axial flow compressors can produce higher compression ratios compared to a centrifugal compressor, they have a greater appeal with manufacturers looking for better fuel efficiency. In helicopters, often both are used together to achieve a good compromise between compressor ratio, specific fuel consumption and reliability.

Centrifugal Compressor

The centrifugal compressor consists of an impeller supported in a casing which houses a ring of diffuser vanes and thence out through a manifold and tubing or ducting into the combustion chamber.

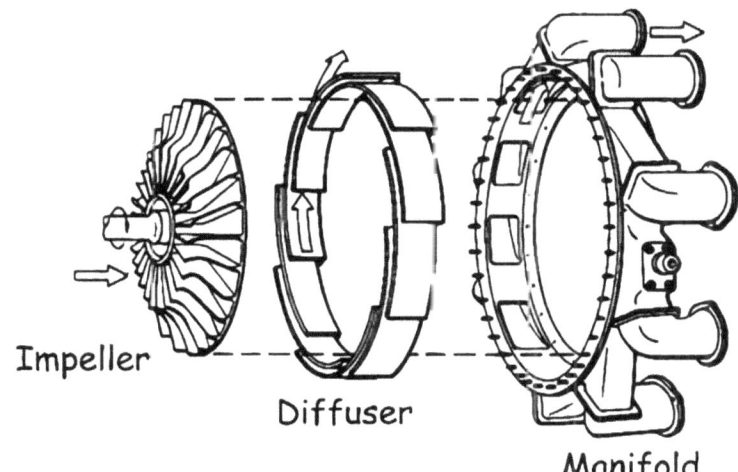

The impeller is driven at high speeds by the turbine through a drive shaft and draws air in through its centre. Centrifugal action forces the air radially outwards and accelerates it into a diverging diffuser outlet. This ring of diffuser blades give direction to the air while decelerating it in the diverging passages, this increases the pressure even more before moving through the manifold and into the combustion chamber. Approximately half the pressure rise is achieved in the impeller and half in the diffuser.

Impeller

The impeller is a forged disc, normally made of an alloy for lightness, with integral radial vanes. When mated together with the compressor cases, the disc and the case form divergent passages. The impeller accelerates air while at the same time increasing its pressure. The impeller tip speed can reach 1600 feet/second (about 950kts) and can rotate around 56000 RPM. The impeller design can include single, double-sided, or even multi-stages.

The single entry which has air drawn by the impeller from the forward side only

The double entry, which has air drawn from both sides of the impeller

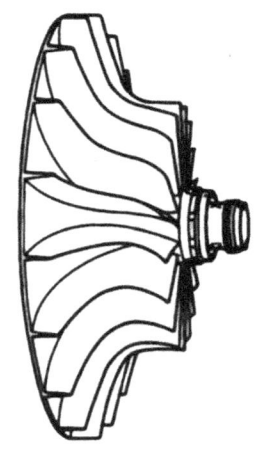
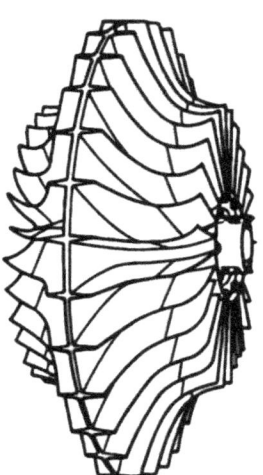

It is also possible to have more than one centrifugal compressor. Each added impeller is called a stage. The diagram below shows a two-stage centrifugal compressor

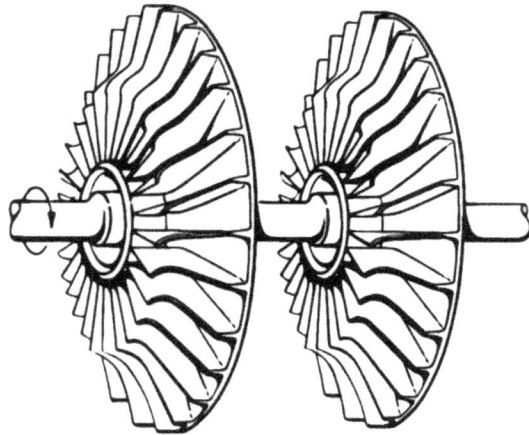

Swirl vanes or inlet guide vanes are often included to direct the intake air onto the centre of the centrifugal compressor impeller at such an angle that the impeller efficiency is increased.

The shaft joining the impeller to the turbine is mounted on bearings and may be a single piece or have joins.

Basic Gas Turbines *for Helicopter Pilots*

Diffuser

Diffuser vanes are shaped like small aerofoils and as the air leaves the impeller tip at high speed it then moves into the diffuser channels (the space between each of the diffuser vanes) where it is re-directed and slowed down so that a substantial portion of the air's velocity is converted into pressure. Of the total compression in a centrifugal compressor, half the pressure rise is produced in the impeller and half in the diffuser.

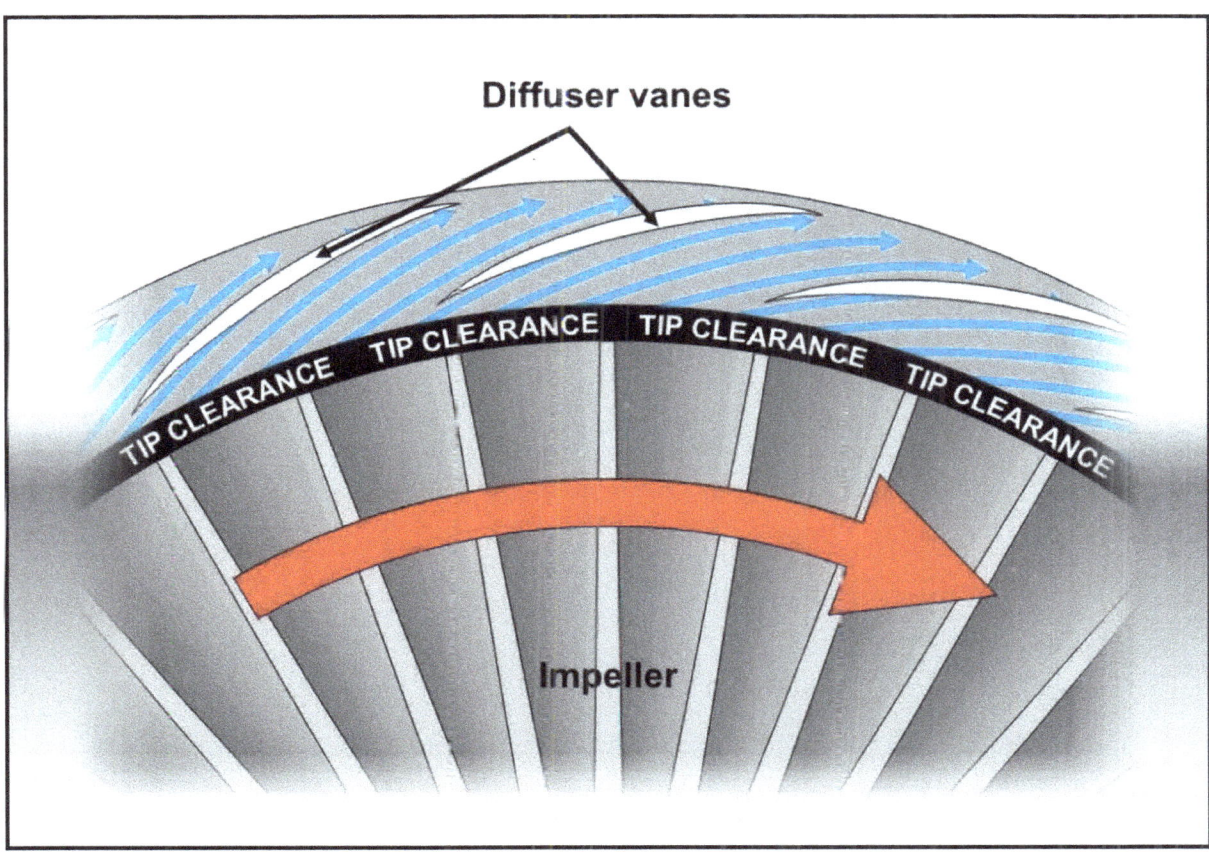

Manifold

The manifold is simply made up of piping or ducting (commonly referred to as transfer tubes) that directs the air coming from the diffuser into the combustion chamber.

Mike Becker, Becker Helicopters

Axial Flow Compressor

This consists of several alternating stages of rotating and stationary aerofoil shaped blades encased in a housing. Each combined set of rotating and stationary blades is known as a stage.

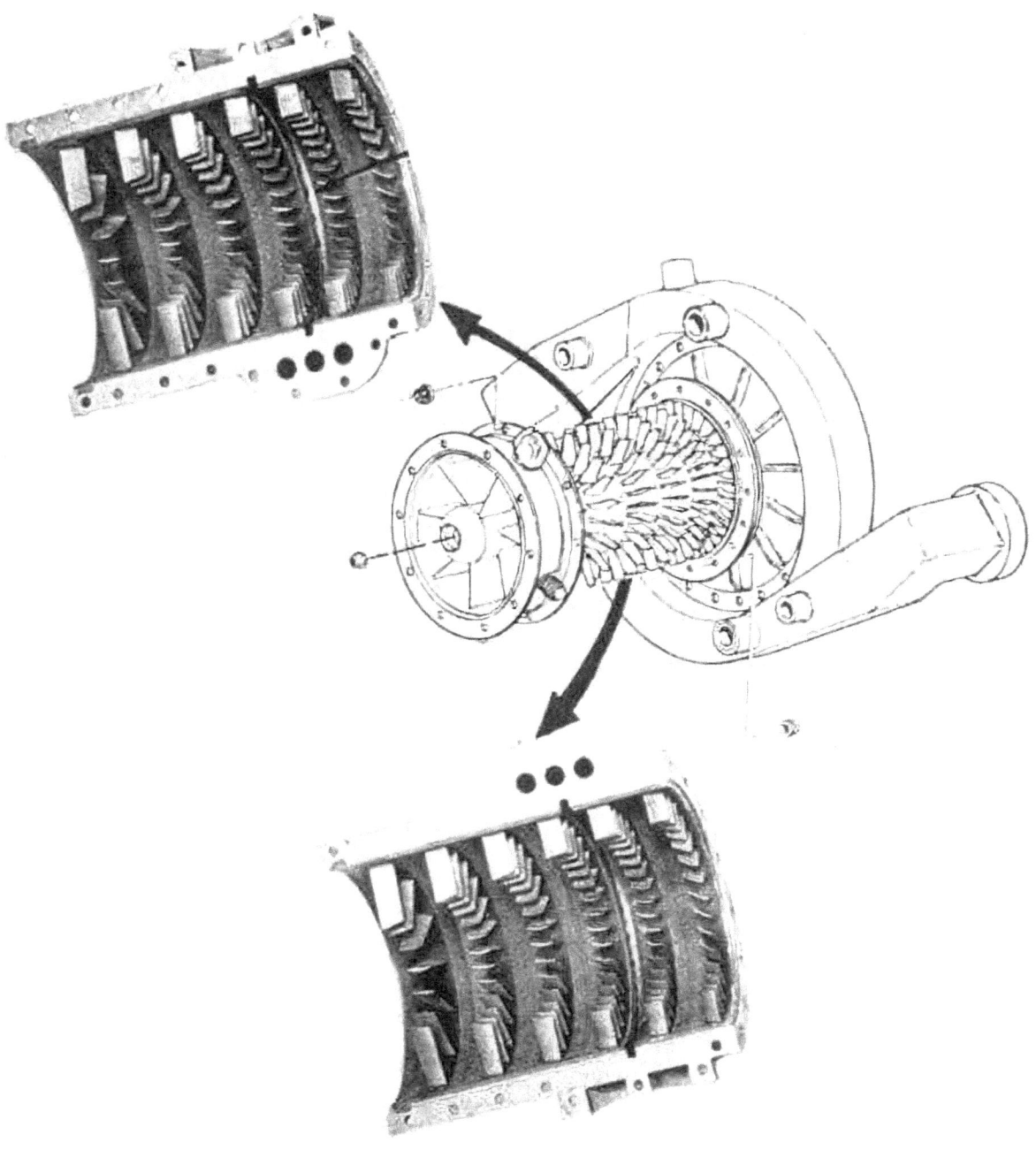

Figure 10 Axial flow compressor with 6 stages

Cascade Effect

As the axial rotor blades spin, they draw air into the system, the air then meets the stationary stator blades which redirect this moving air onto the next axial rotor blade at the most efficient angle. The aerofoils are arranged in a cascade. This means that the aerofoils are arranged one after the other which influences air under low pressure in the front stages to flow into an area of higher pressure. The ability of air to flow rearward against an ever-increasing pressure is similar to forcing water to flow uphill.

Looking at the pressure zones on an aerofoil, if a slight positive angle of attack exists, there is a high-pressure present on the bottom of the aerofoil when compared to the top of the aerofoil.

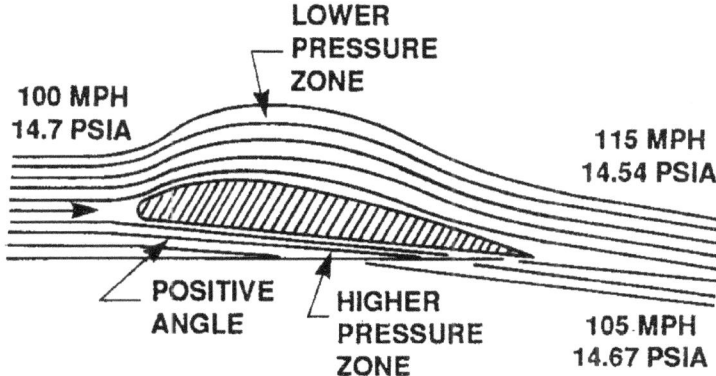

These high- and low-pressure zones apply to both the rotating (rotors) and the stationary (stators) aerofoils and allow the air in one set of aerofoils (stage) to come under the influence of the next set. This is known as the cascade effect.

High-pressure air from the first stage is pumped into the low-pressure zone of its stator.

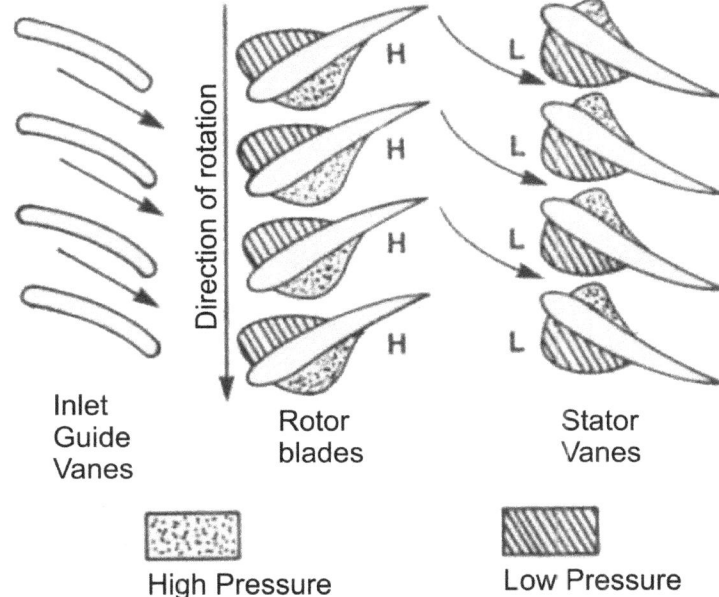

Each stage is also in a converging duct this will reduce the velocity and increase the pressure. The pressure is gradually built up as the air passes through the compressor stages until it reaches the combustion chamber.

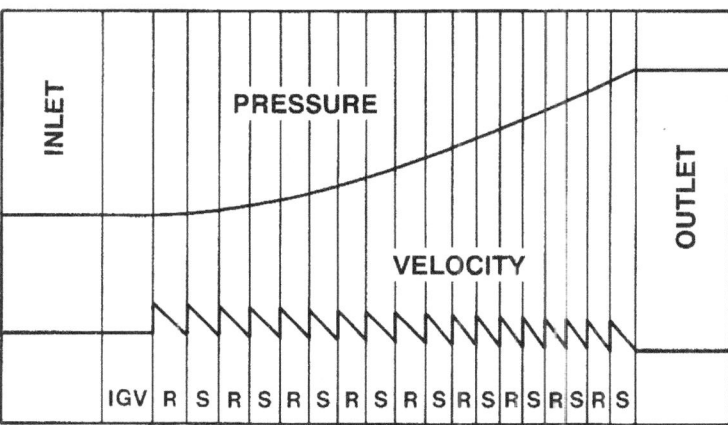

The rotating blades are carried on discs or a drum driven by a driveshaft connected to the turbine. The stationary blades or "stator" blades are connected to the outer casing to form a stator row. (Commonly called a row of stator vanes.)

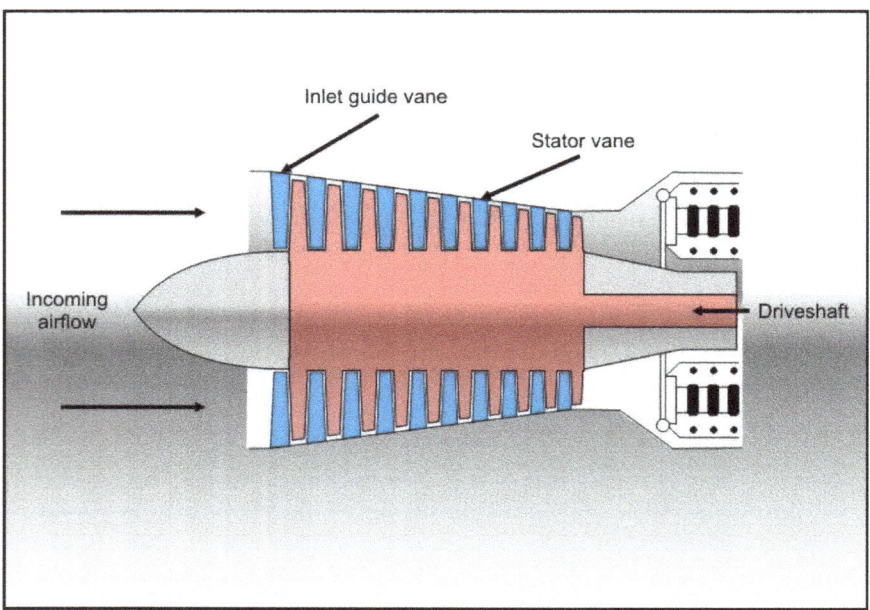

Because of the very fine design tolerances in an Axial compressor, they are very prone to getting dirty and/or damaged.

Rotor Blades

The axial flow compressor rotor blades are spinning at a very high velocity (approximately 56000 RPM) therefore they experience very high centrifugal loads and very high tip speeds.

Compressor rotor blade attachment

The rotors must be securely attached to the rotating disc or drum which are themselves bolted or welded together and connected to the driveshaft.

The three main methods of attaching the rotors to the discs are as follows:

Retaining pin and lock	**Fir-tree root and locking plate**	**Dovetail root and locking screw**

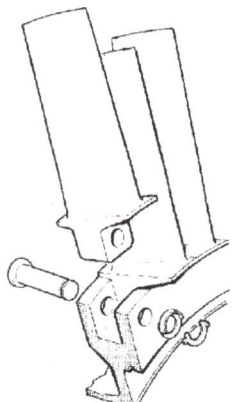 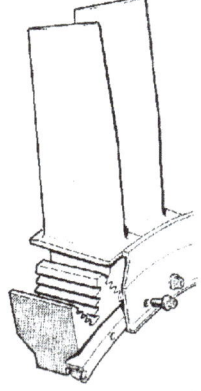 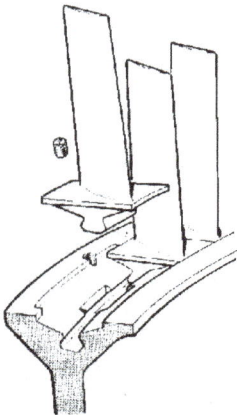

Stagger angle

As air flow moves through the axial compressor, each stage must deal with airflow characteristics that are different from the previous or following stage. To cater for this, each stage can be designed differently with rotor blade angles or 'stagger angles' varying over the length of the rotor blade.

Each rotor blade is machined to specific aerofoil shapes with a very high degree of accuracy in manufacture. The twist provides a pressure gradient along the span of the blade, producing a uniform velocity of axial flow.

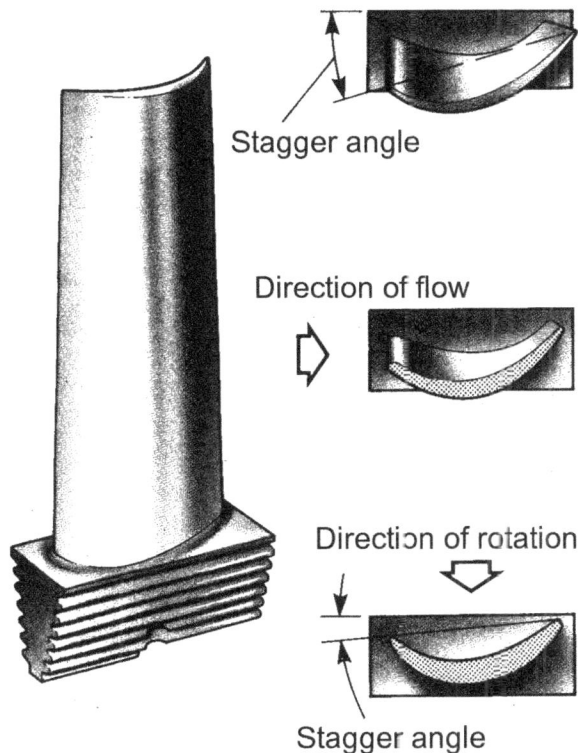

The twist given to a set of rotor blades on a stage would be suitable for only that stage therefore the designer must carefully assess the needs of each stage and adjust the twist to match the needs of the compressor.

Stator Vanes

Stator vanes have an aerofoil shape and are attached to the outer casing of the compressor. They may be attached directly as single units or assembled in retaining rings which are then attached to the outer case in segments or stages.

The compressor case which carries the stator vanes may be assembled around the rotor blades by joining two halves or they may be made up of several short cylinders and bolted together.

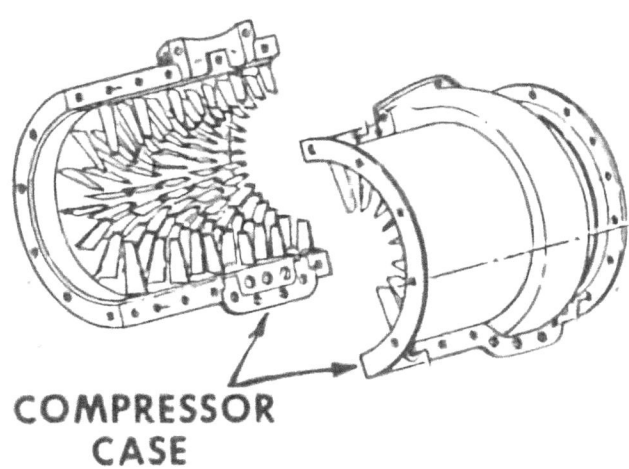

COMPRESSOR CASE

Combined Axial and Centrifugal Compressor

Below is an example of a Rolls Royce C20 combined axial and centrifugal compressor section. Showing six stages of axial compression and one stage of centrifugal compression.

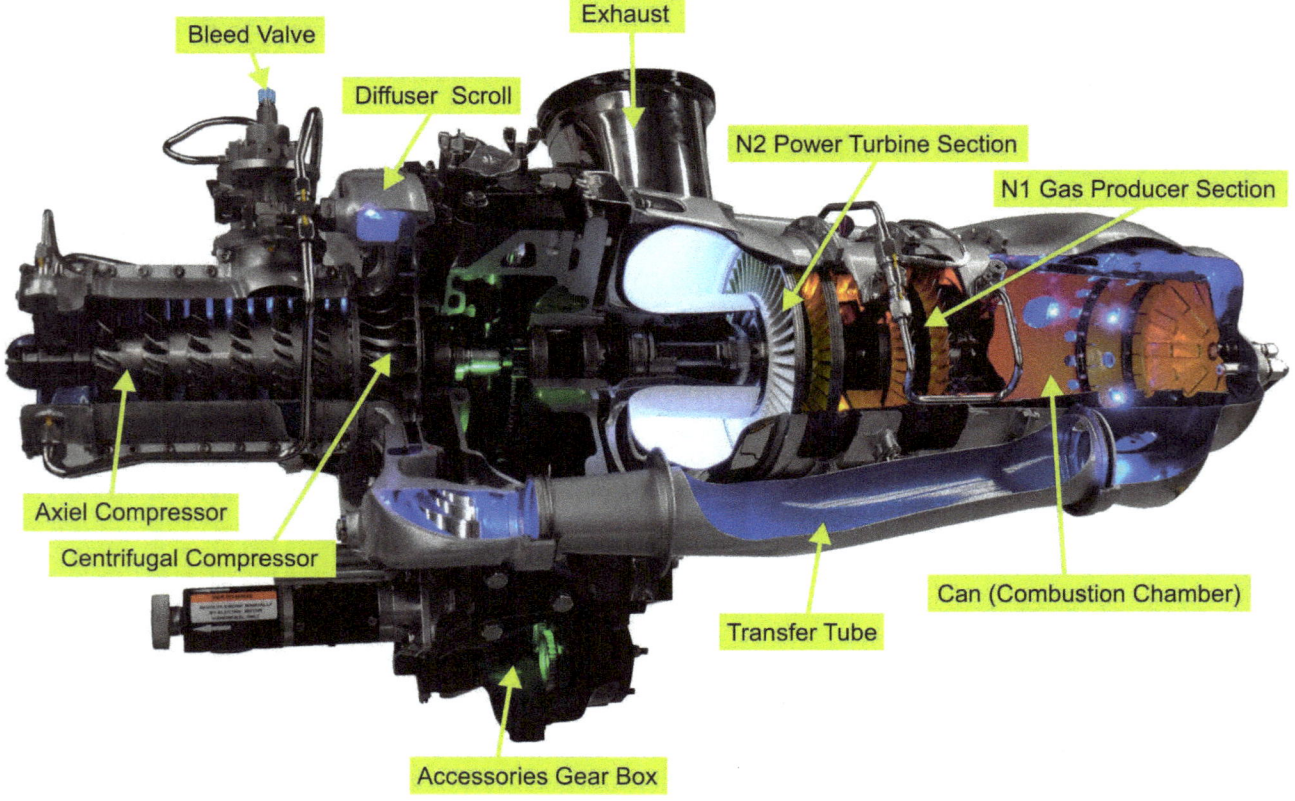

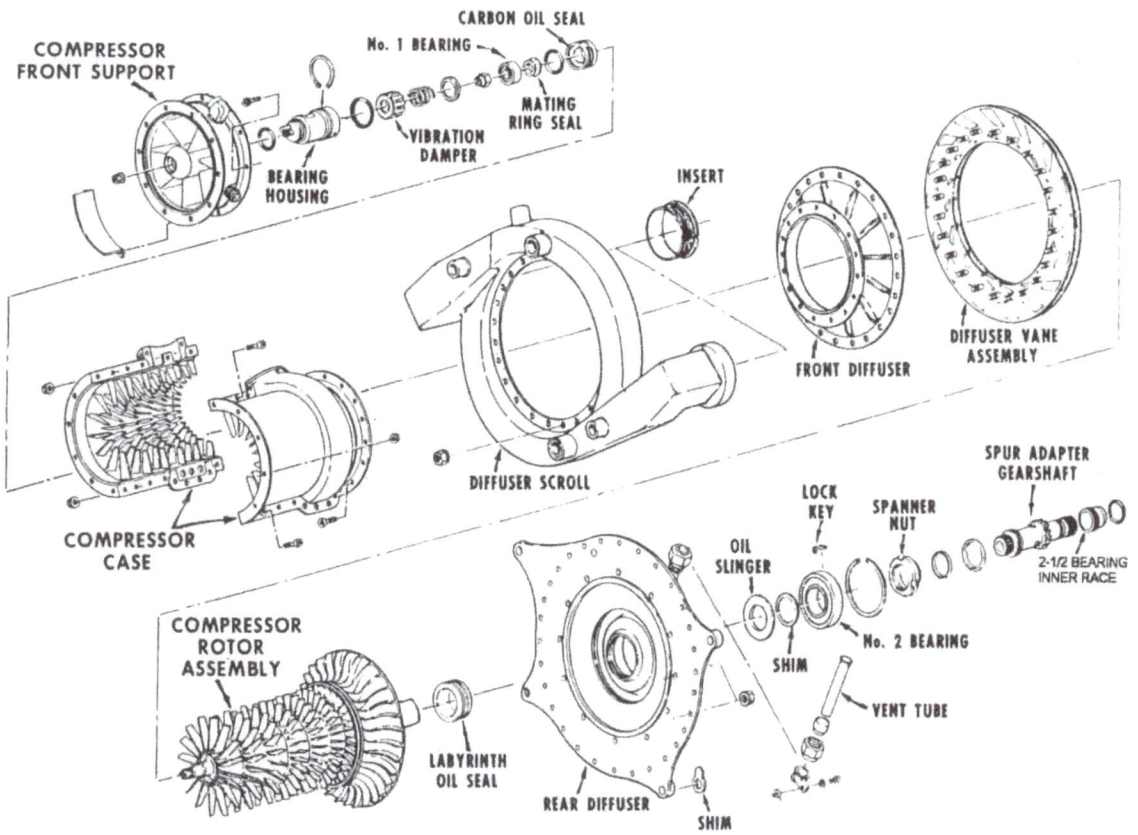

Basic Gas Turbines *for Helicopter Pilots*

Airflow through the Engine

Following is a diagram showing the flow of air through the Rolls Royce C20 turbine engine.

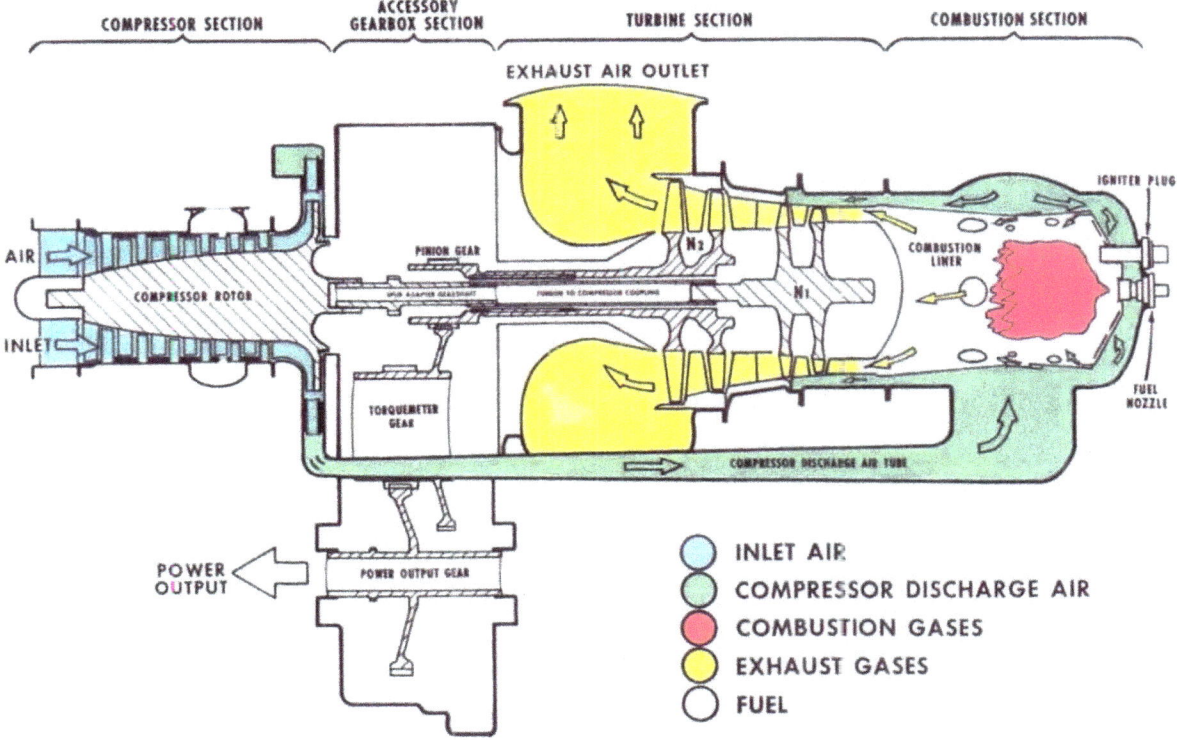

Airflow Control

Because of the high-pressure ratios required from a single shaft, it is not always possible to maintain "design" RPM (especially during start and idle). Therefore, manufacturers included features into their compressor designs to manipulate the airflow to its best potential and to keep the correct angle of attack.

Variable Inlet Guide Vanes

These are found at the front of the compressor. The relative airflow into the engine can be directed onto the first stage at the correct angle of attack in various operating conditions to prevent surge and stall of the compressor blades. These inlet guide vanes can change their angle of attack by moving. This is done automatically by an actuator arm receiving information from air pressure sensors at various engine RPM.

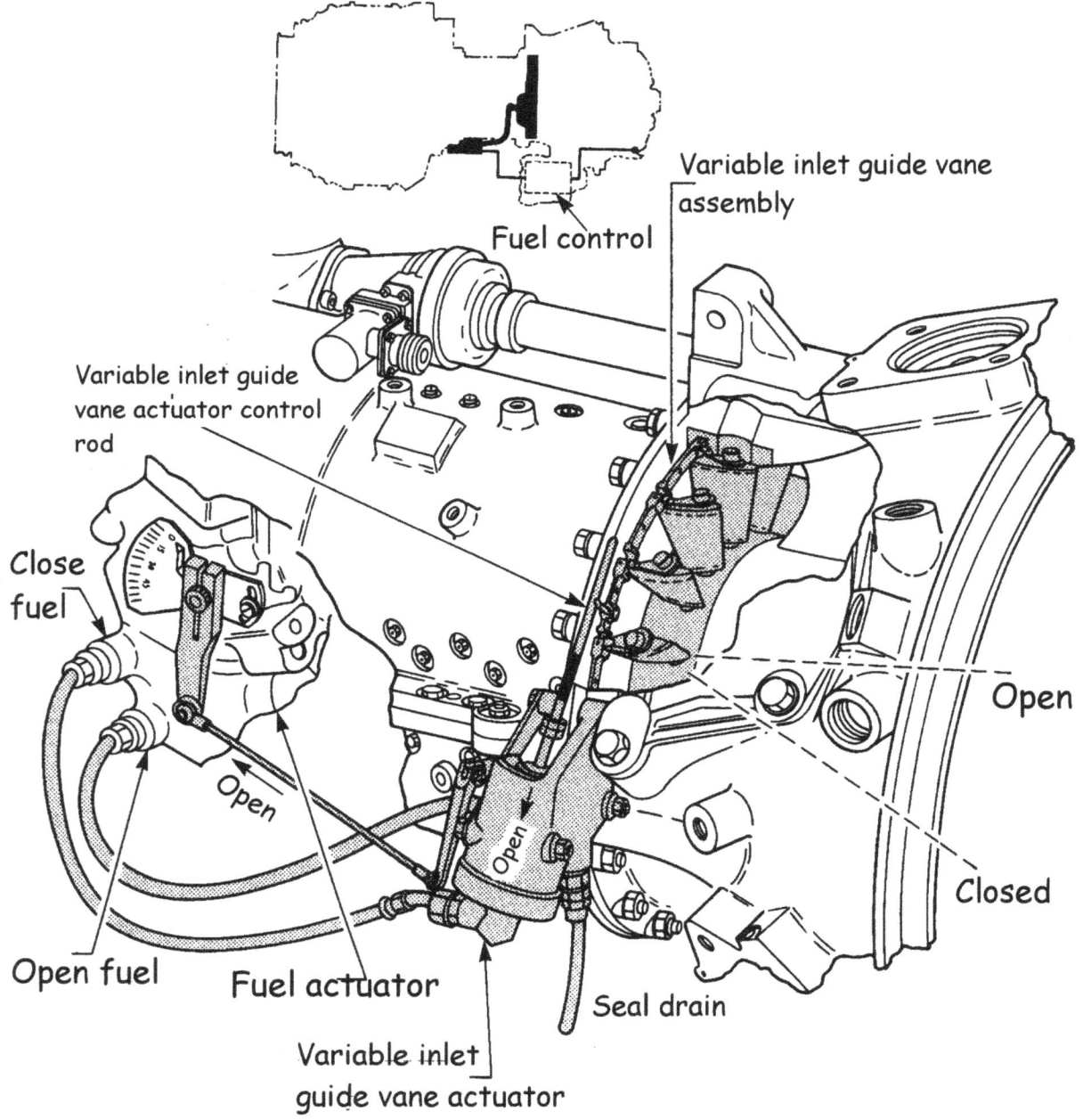

Variable Stator Vanes

Can vary the airflow direction in-between stages to maintain the correct angle of attack when the engine is operating off its design RPM. Again these variable stator vanes can change their angle of attack by moving. This is done automatically by an actuator arm receiving information from air pressure sensors at various engine RPM.

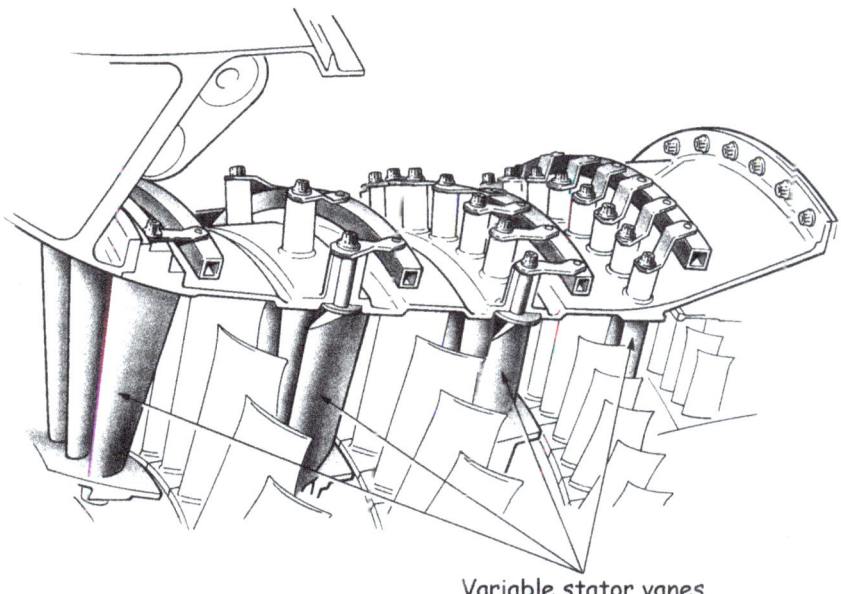
Variable stator vanes

Bleed Air Valve

Since the power demands from the turbine engine may vary, there will be times when the compressor section produces more air than is needed by the combustor. The bleed air system then opens to release this excess air before it travels through to the combustor and therefore reduces the back pressure. The bleed valve helps reduce the possibility of the compressor stalling.

Figure 11 Bleed air valve on the C20B turbine engine

Different designs may be used to increase or decrease the bleed air flow dependent on demand. Some designs use a flow fence actuator which is a small ring around the outside of the compressor casing that opens and closes dependent on demand, others use a bleed valve that opens and closes based on air pressure sensors through the fuel control unit.

Example of a bleed band system

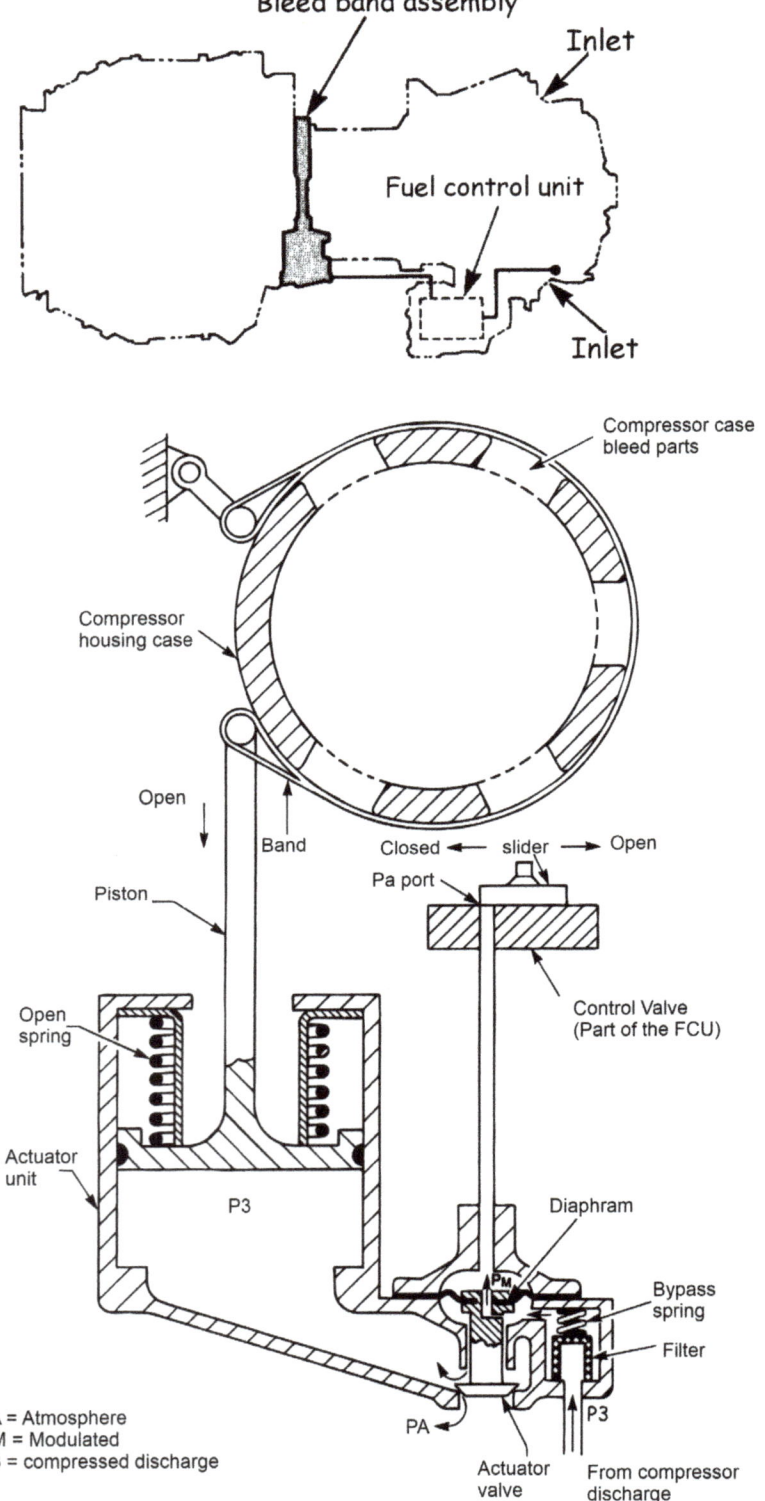

PA = Atmosphere
PM = Modulated
P3 = compressed discharge

Basic Gas Turbines *for Helicopter Pilots*

Example of a bleed valve system

On the C20B, the bleed valve is open for the start and gradually closes as N1 RPM increases. Around 93% N1, it is fully closed. It can open briefly to aid accelerations.

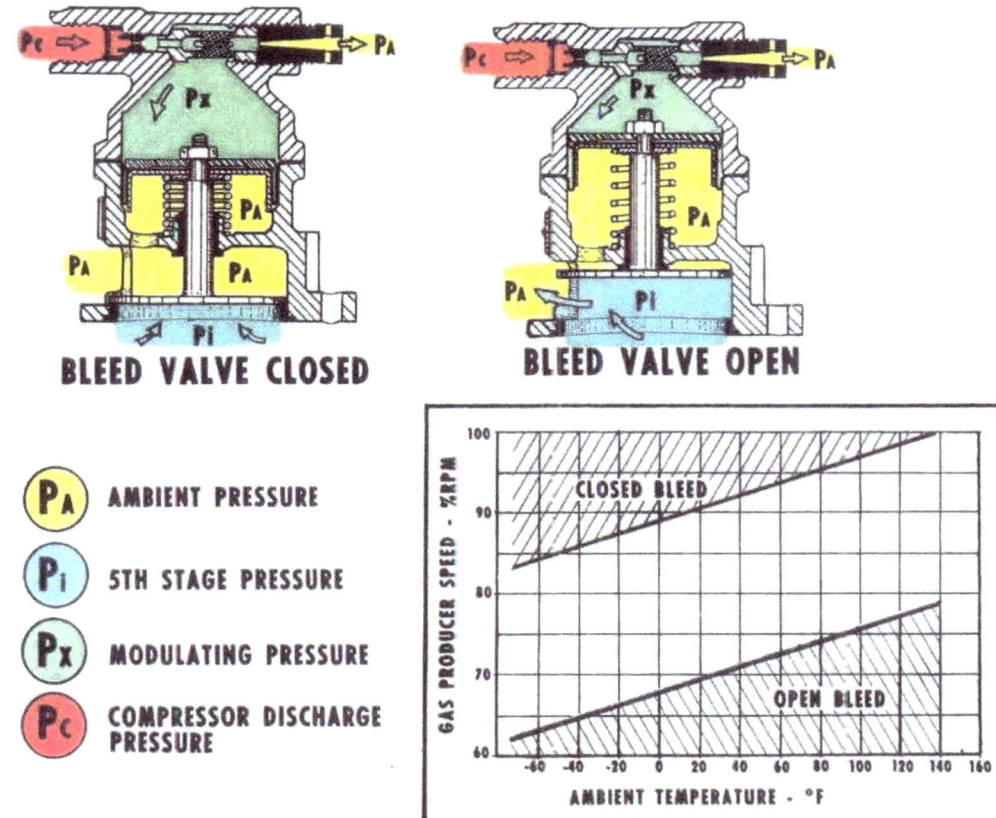

Bleed air for accessories

Bleed air is stored energy that is surplus to requirements, therefore it is 'bled off' the system. It is common for the manufacturer to utilise this air to drive other systems.

In helicopters, bleed air is commonly used as an anti-ice and de-icing system and to drive the environmental control system (ECS), in other words, the heater and the air conditioner.

If intake ice is detected the pilot can activate the de-ice system, this directs some of the hot bleed air onto the intake to melt the ice.

Anti-ice switch in a Jet Ranger   **Anti-ice system actuator arm on the compressor**

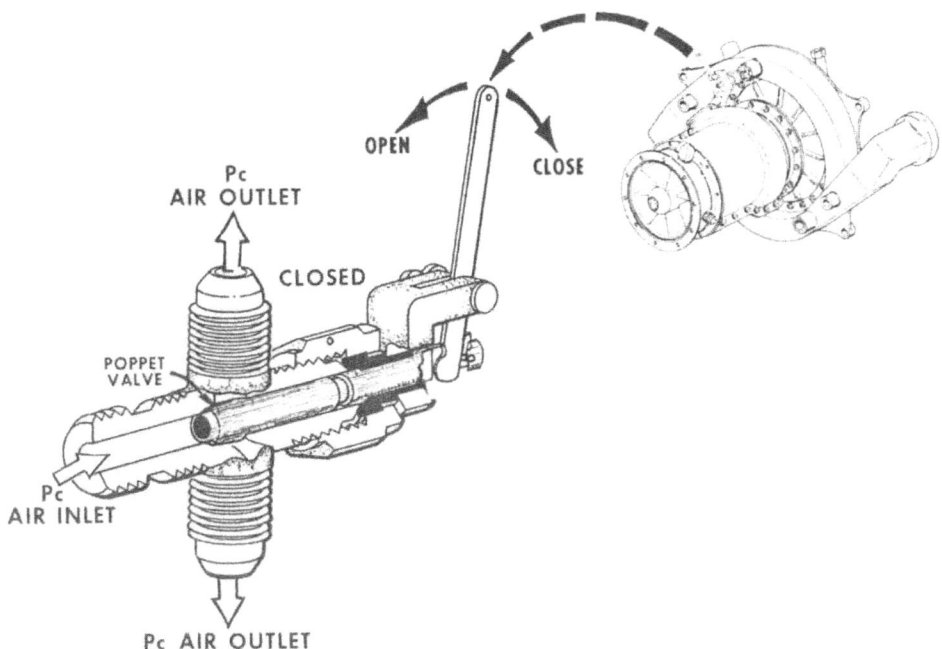

Figure 12 Schematic of a bleed air actuator arm

If the pilot activates the ECS, this directs bleed air into a heat exchanger, this is basically a small turbine that processes air to either heat it up or cool it down for use in the cabin for crew and passenger comfort.

The disadvantage of using bleed air for these systems is twofold:

- Air is taken out of the system; therefore turbine temperatures will increase due to less air being available for cooling, and
- In the case of the de-icing system, hot air is directed at the intake, therefore compressor temperatures will be higher, leading again to an increase in turbine temperatures.

When pilots are operating at high-density altitudes where turbine temperatures are close to the limits and may even be limiting torque, then the activation of the bleed air system may cause a further limitation or even cause limits to be exceeded, so pilots need to be very aware of how they manage the bleed air system for accessories in a turbine engine.

Compressor Stalls and Surging

The terms compressor stall and compressor surging have similar meanings with one leading to the other in a cascading problem.

Since an axial flow compressor essentially consists of a series of small stationery (stator vanes) and rotating (rotor blade) aerofoil sections, the aerodynamic rules that apply to an aerofoil (wing or rotor blade) will also apply to the blades and vanes in a compressor.

Basic Gas Turbines *for Helicopter Pilots*

A compressor stall is when there is a disruption over one of the rotating blades due to an increase in the angle of attack beyond the critical angle. This will have a cascading effect in that once one rotor blade stalls so does the next one and so on.

Normal blade angle

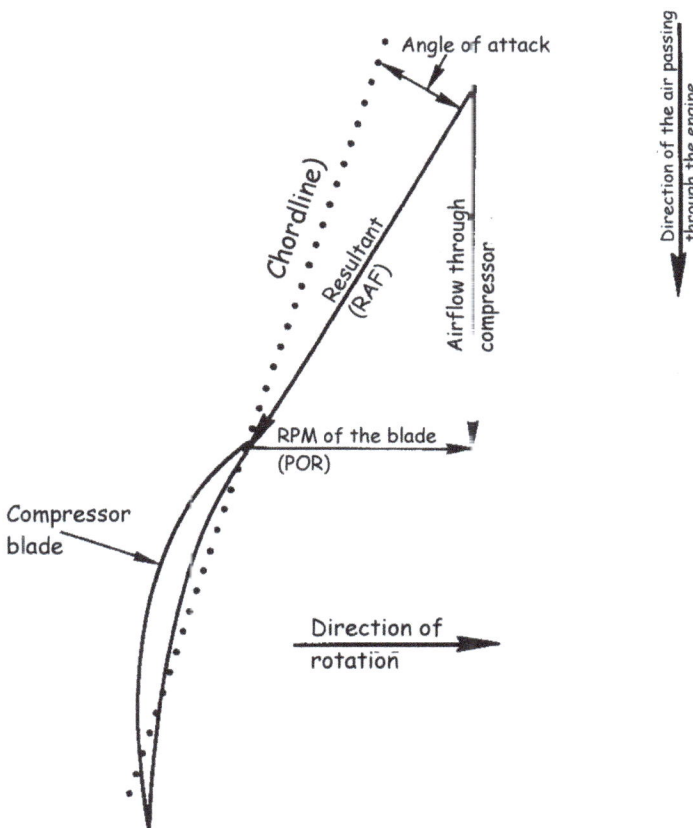

Stalled blade angle

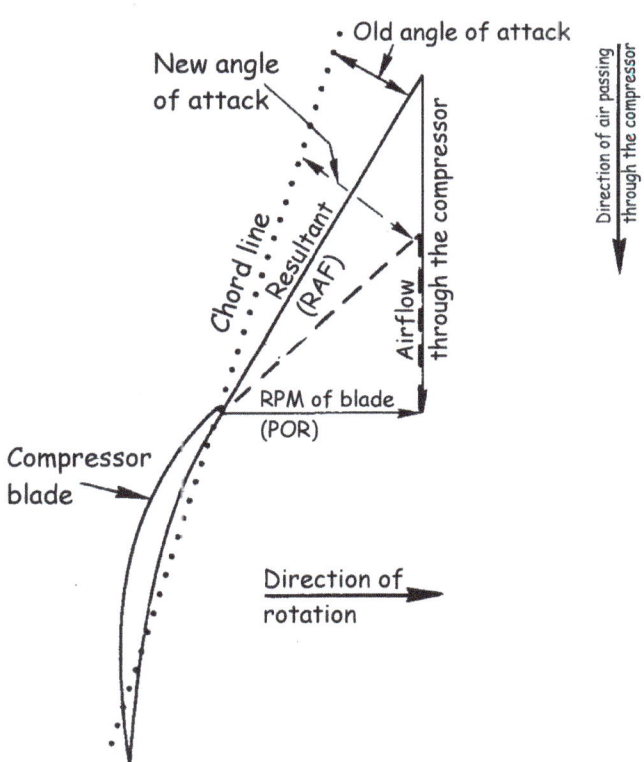

This leads to a loss of compressor pressure and the gas from the combustion chamber can surge back through the compressor.

The main variables that affect the angle of attack of the airflow in the compressor blades are the velocity of the airflow and the engine RPM. In helicopters, the velocity of airflow and engine RPM is normally constant and therefore compressor stall and surge is not normally a function of a pilot mishandling the engine management. It is usually a result of:

- Dirty rotors and stators.
- Damaged rotors or stators.
- Fuel control unit problems.
- Bleed valve problems.
- Leakage in the engine plumbing from the compressor to the combustor.
- A problem at the intake including a damaged intake filter, ice, or blockage.
- N1 topping. This is where the compressor is asked to work beyond its limits.

Symptoms of compressor stall or surge

A compressor stall of only 1 or 2 stages will normally be accompanied by a low rumble that can be heard in the cockpit. The pilot may also notice torque, TOT and N1 surges, accompanied by small oscillations in the tail as the TQ surges.

A complete compressor stall leading to a compressor surge produces an explosive noise, similar to a shotgun going off in the engine. It can be violent and very distinct.

When a full-blown stall and compressor surge is in progress, the stalling reduces the compressor discharge pressure below the combustion chamber pressure and as a result, the hot expanding gases (flame) move in the wrong direction shooting from the combustor forward back through the compressor.

The obvious symptoms to the pilot are:

- A loud banging or pop pop popping sound (similar to a gun going off in the engine bay) coming from the engine.
- Torque fluctuations on both the TQ gauge as well as tail yaw oscillations.
- In severe cases, vibration in the cockpit to the point that gauges may not be able to be read.
- Rapidly rising TOT.
- Fluctuating engine RPM.
- Fluctuating N1.
- In severe cases that are allowed to continue, reducing RRPM to the point of the low RPM horn sounding.

Remedy for a compressor stall

Prevention is better than the cure in this case, so to avoid a compressor stall:

- Do regular compressor washes before a flight.
- Avoid damage to the compressor by installing a particle separator or air intake filter or at least avoid operations with FOD, particularly sand.
- Any hint of an FCU problem have it looked at by an engineer.
- Any unusual rise in operating TOT may be indicative of a Bleed valve problem or a leak in the manifold, again have an engineer look at it early.
- Be aware of your in-flight conditions, plan and fly accordingly. This includes operating within the manufacturers' limitations, in a helicopter, this is often overlooked at altitude, or in adverse weather conditions, where pilots top out the N1 and encounter a compressor stall.
- A problem at the intake including a damaged intake filter, ice, or blockage.
- If you do encounter a compressor stall or surge, then **lower the collective**. In most cases, this is all you need to do to recover from the stall. You may lower it only a small amount or you may have to lower it all the way, a lot will depend on what the initial cause was. Once the stall has gone and the turbine again runs smoothly, re-introduce the collective enough to recover and return to base or landing. This is the normal outcome for a compressor stall.
- If the stall continues then you may have to enter autorotation and conduct an emergency forced landing. This is not the normal outcome for a compressor stall in a helicopter.

Damage due to compressor stalls

The engine does not usually suffer any permanent damage after a compressor stall; however in a helicopter, because of the abrupt and large TQ changes, damage may be sustained to the drive train. In particular, the tail rotor gearbox is put under a lot of pressure.

During or after a severe compressor stall do not be surprised if the tail rotor chip light comes on necessitating a landing and inspection.

Also, have a good look at all of the drive shaft couplings and flex plates for stressing.

Because of the large vibrations that may be experienced in the cockpit, it is also not uncommon for gauges, instruments and radios to fail or be damaged.

Combustion Section

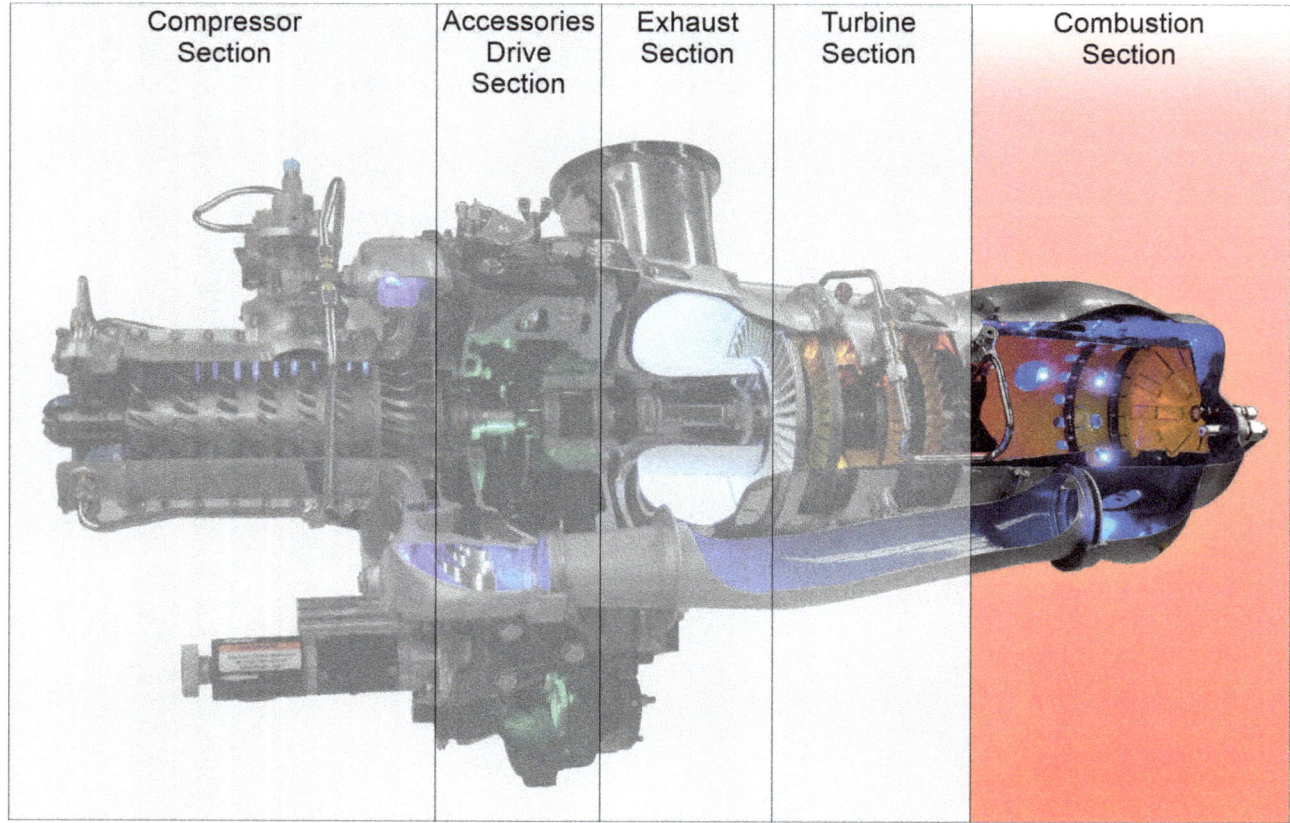

The combustion chamber has the job of burning large amounts of fuel, supplied from the fuel spray nozzles, with extensive volumes of air supplied by the compressor. It then releases the heat energy in such a manner that the air is expanded and accelerated to give a smooth stream of uniformly heated gas at all operating conditions required to rotate the turbine.

The amount of fuel added to the air will depend on the rise in temperature that is required to produce the shaft horsepower at the turbine. The maximum temperature is limited by the materials that make up the turbine blades and nozzles. This is in the range of 850 degrees to 1700 degrees, so design methods are required to keep the heat away from the surface of the materials.

Combustion Chamber

The combustion chamber consists of an outer casing, an inner perforated liner, a fuel injection system and a starting ignition system.

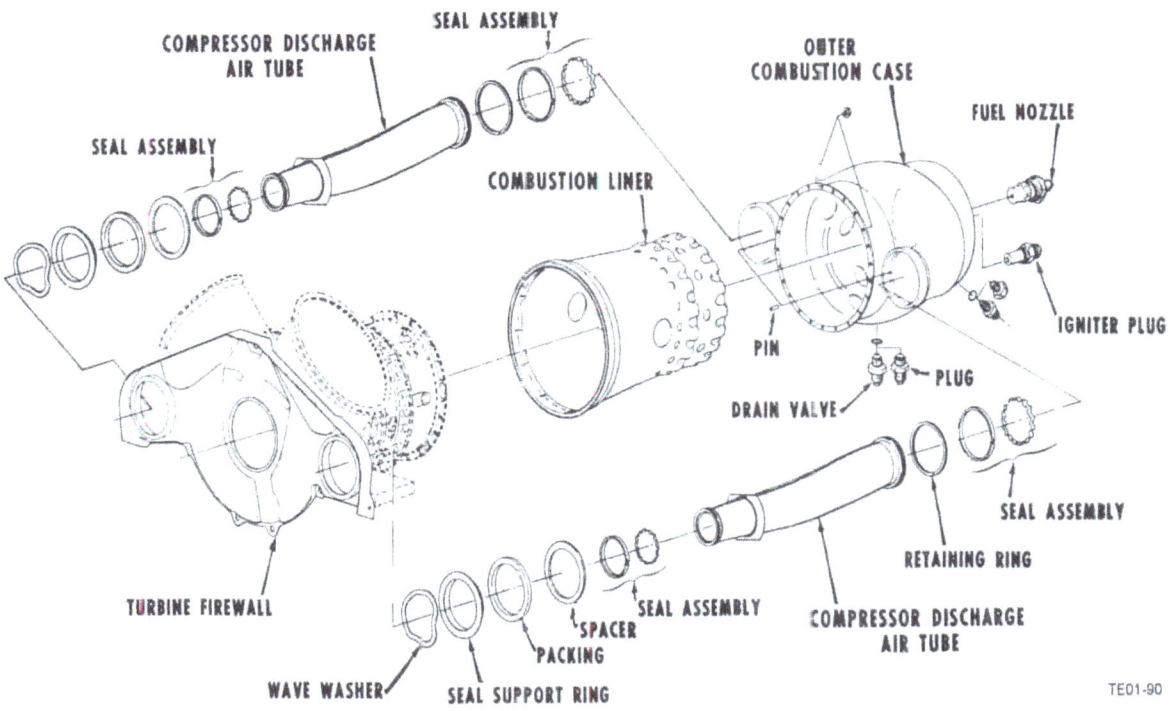

The components of the combustion chamber can be further described in the following generic diagram.

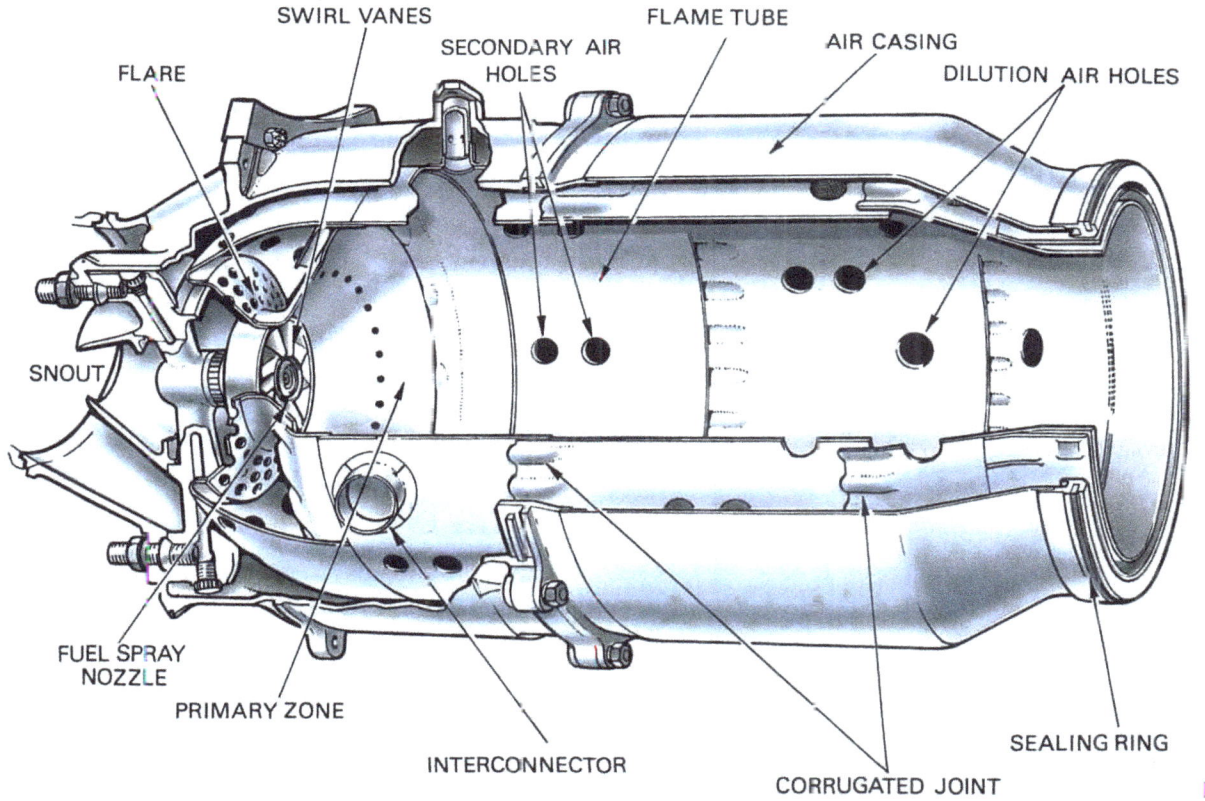

Combustion occurs in a gas turbine engine at constant pressure, so construction can be of light materials. The ideal mixture of air to fuel is 15:1.

Combustion Chamber Airflow

Compressor air enters the combustion chamber at velocities up to 500 feet/sec and at temperatures already around 200° to 500°C. Kerosene will not burn in an airflow of over 80 feet/sec, therefore a region of low air velocity is needed to keep the flame alight, and so for this purpose, the front section of the combustion chamber is used to decelerate some of the air.

The flame must be 'anchored' in this slower moving air and in many engines, the fuel nozzle provides this anchor by delivering the fuel under pressure to a particular area in the centre of the can. Once the fuel is ignited it adds a further 500° to 700°C in the combustion process. This is a total gas turbine temperature of around 700° to 1200°C. The highest temperature of gases involved in the combustion process is at the flame itself, of approximately 2300°C.

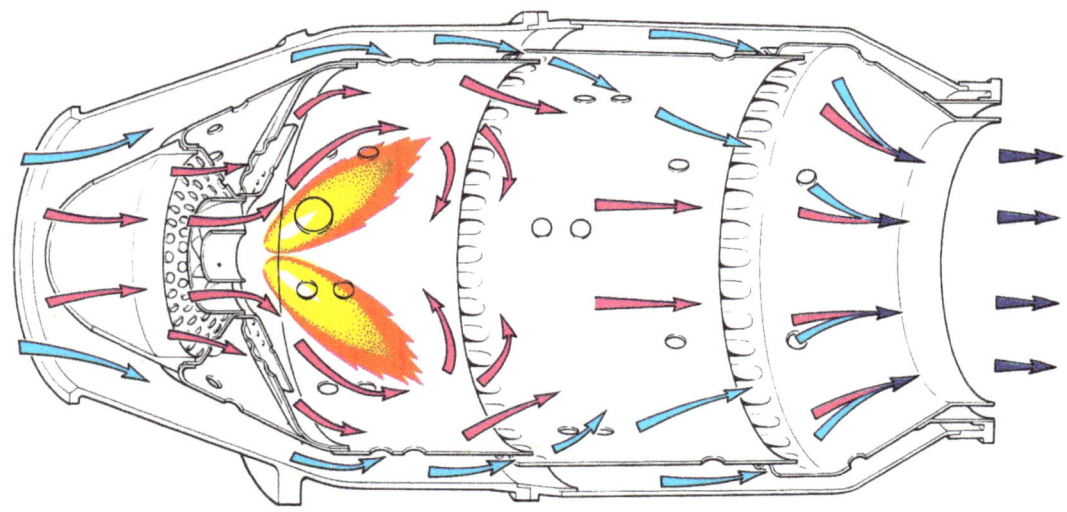

[9]

Only 20% of the total air takes part in the combustion process. This is called Primary air. Primary air enters then passes by the swirl vanes and the perforated flare to the primary combustion zone. Swirl vanes reduce the velocity of the primary air and keep the flame stabilized in the primary zone, ensuring an even mixture of fuel and air. The ignited swirling mixture is combined with a further 20% of total air, which enters through holes in the flame tube walls. The result is that combustion is completed, and the remainder of the secondary air is used to cool the flame tube walls and the hot gas temperature, additionally, this expanding gas will add to the useful power.

The remaining 60% of the total air is used solely for cooling. It is introduced progressively into the flame tube to cool the gases in the dilution zone, and to form an insulation layer against the flame tube walls.

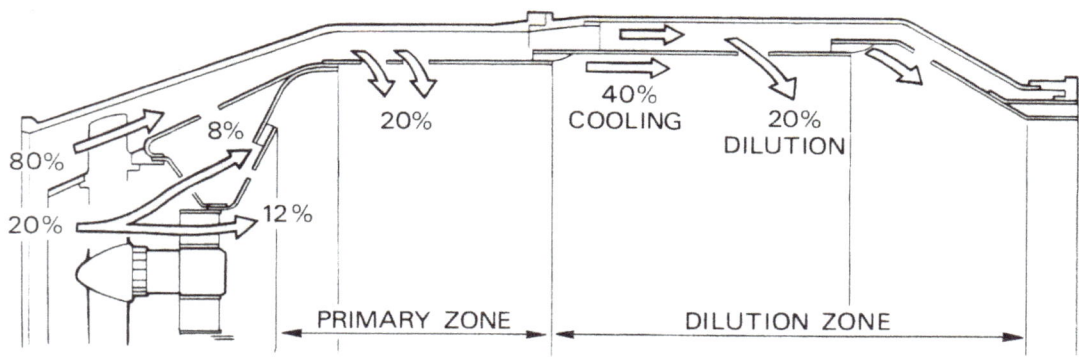

Ignition of the mixture is supplied by electric igniter plug/s. Once it is burning, the flame is self-sustaining which means it continuously burns. Fuel is supplied to the airstream as a finely atomised spray from the fuel spray nozzle. The turbulent airflow aids mixing.

Flame out

Flame out, due to a lean mixture, may occur at low fuel pressures, with low engine speeds at high altitude flight. In these circumstances, a weak mixture is set up that can easily be blown out even at normal airflows.

Flame out due to a rich mixture may occur during very fast engine acceleration in which an over-rich mixture is present that causes a rise in combustion pressure until the compressor airflow stagnates. The interruption to the normally continuous airflow may cause flame extinction.

Flame out is normally designed out of the system under normal operating parameters.

Types of Combustion Chamber

There are a few different types of combustion chambers in use. These are:

- The can,
- The annular, and
- The can-annular types.

Can or Multiple-Can

This older type of combustor is not commonly used today. It consists of multiple outer housings, each with its own perforated liner and is mostly found on engines with a centrifugal compressor. Air leaving the diffuser is divided and ducted into individual combustor cans. There is a fuel nozzle and a burner liner in each can.

Each of the separate cans is its own burner unit, but they all discharge their hot gases into one open area at the turbine nozzle inlet.

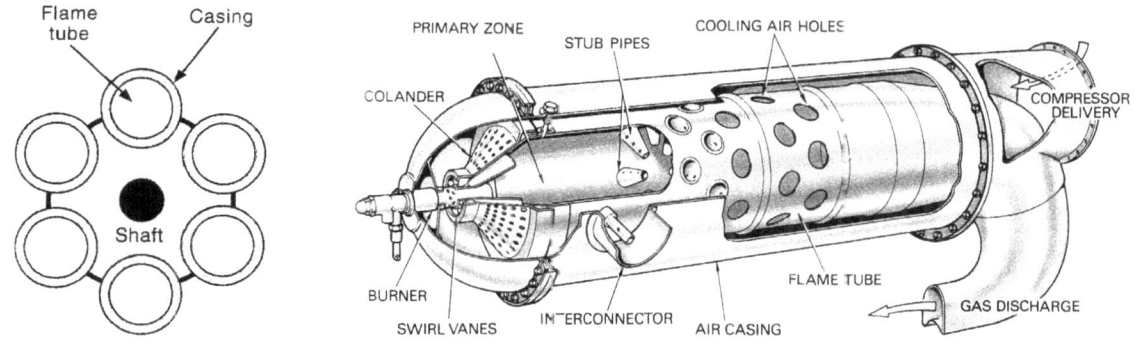

Advantages of the multiple can type

- Service life is good, in other words, they last for a reasonable amount of time before being replaced.
- The individual cans can be removed for inspection or replacement without having to take out the entire engine.
- Each can, or combustion chamber is light weight and of sturdy construction.

Annular

The annular type of combustion chamber is used often with axial flow compressors. Annular means "ring-like" shape. There is a single flame tube, made up of an inner and outer housing. The chamber is open to the compressor at the front and to the turbine nozzles at the rear. Fuel is introduced using several nozzles located at the upstream end of the combustor. Primary and secondary air provide for combustion and cooling similar to other designs of combustors.

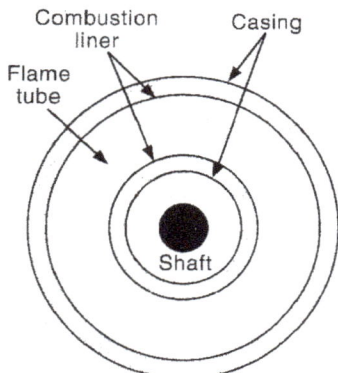

Advantages of the annular type

- It is said to be the best design for thermal efficiency.
- It is located between the compressor and the turbine at about the same diameter as the blades. This provides an engine of minimum size.
- It has minimal surface area exposed to the gas so less cooling is required and less pressure is lost through combustion than in other types.

A disadvantage of the annular type

- A difficulty associated with these is providing adequate cooling air to the internal surfaces of the engine and bearings. This space is completely enclosed.
- This chamber is more difficult and costly to develop than other designs.

Can-Annular

Individual cans are placed side by side to form a circle of cans inside an annular chamber. The cans are essentially individual combustion chambers with rings of perforated holes in the walls to admit cooling air. Fuel nozzles are located around the forward end of each can. Because the cans are of a relatively small diameter, they are strong and have a high degree of heat distortion resistance. A flame tube is found at the forward end of the can. This tube allows propagation of flame and equal internal pressures between the separate cans.

The can-annular type of combustion chamber combines the advantages of both the can and the annular types. It also eliminates many of their disadvantages. A removable shroud (or a telescoping one) covers the entire burner assembly. This allows access to the individual cans for removal or inspection.

A short burner length prevents excessive pressure drop of gases between the compressor outlet and the flame area. The design provides an even temperature distribution at the turbine inlet, which minimises the risk of hot spots.

Multiple can-annular combustion chambers

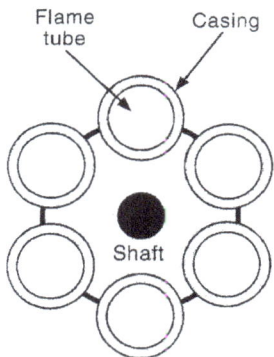

Turbine Section

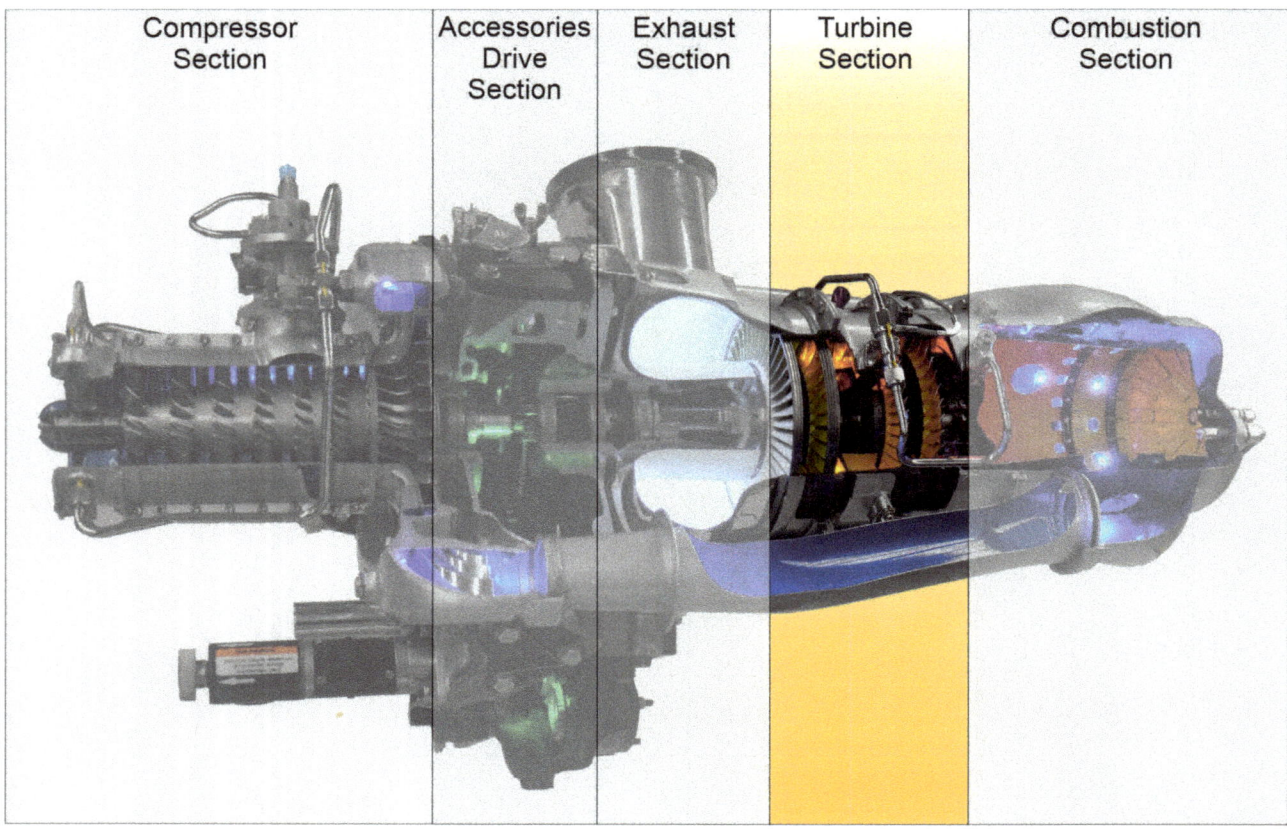

In a pure turbine jet engine, the purpose of the turbine is to extract enough energy to drive the compressor and leave the rest of the **thrust** to propel the aircraft forward. In a turboshaft turbine engine, such as used in helicopters, the purpose of the turbine is to extract the energy from the expanding gases and convert them to **shaft horsepower**. This shaft horsepower can then be used not only to provide power to the compressor and accessories but to drive the transmission via the accessories gearbox in the engine and, therefore, the rotor blades.

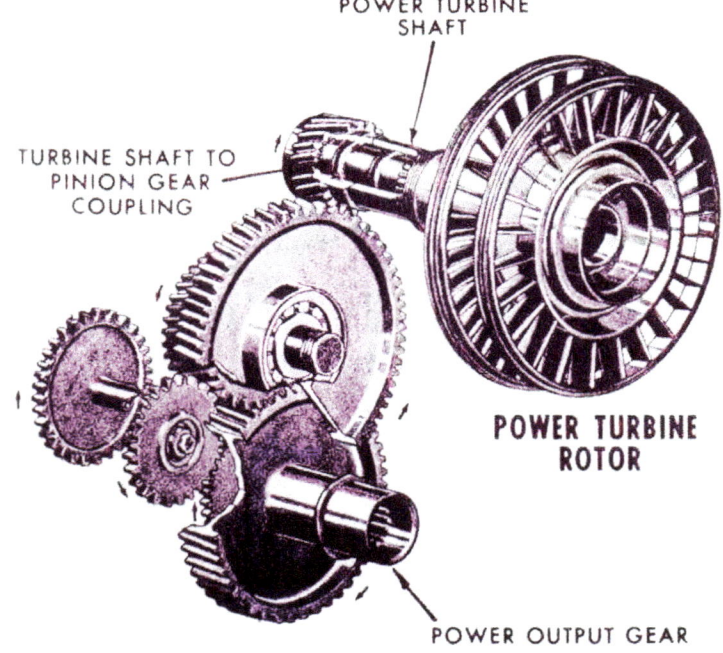

Basic Gas Turbines *for Helicopter Pilots*

As the hot expanding gases leave the combustion chamber, they move into the turbine section. Very similar to the compressor, the turbine section is made up of a series of stationary and rotating aerofoils. The stationary sections are called **nozzle guide vanes** and the rotating sections are called the **rotating turbines**.

Each set of stationary and rotating turbines form a turbine section, each section, through clever design, can run at different RPMs so that the drive shaft connected to them can run at its optimum RPM for the accessory being driven.

The low-pressure turbine will drive the low-pressure compressor, often referred to as the Gas Producer Turbine or N1 (first turbine) as it produces the 'gas' via the compressor for the engine.

The high-pressure turbine will supply power to the driveshaft connected to the accessories gearbox for power. Often referred to then as the 'power' turbine' or N2 (second turbine) as it produces the power used by the rotor system and accessories. This turbine is also referred to as the 'free' turbine as it runs independently of the Gas Producer turbine.

Different turbine engine designs may have 1, 2, 3, 4 or more turbine sections or stages. They may do different jobs or help each other in doing the same job. For example, the first turbine section often only powers the compressor. The remaining turbine sections then combine to provide power to the rotor system.

The following diagrams are of a Rolls Royce 250C20 engine that has two turbine sections.

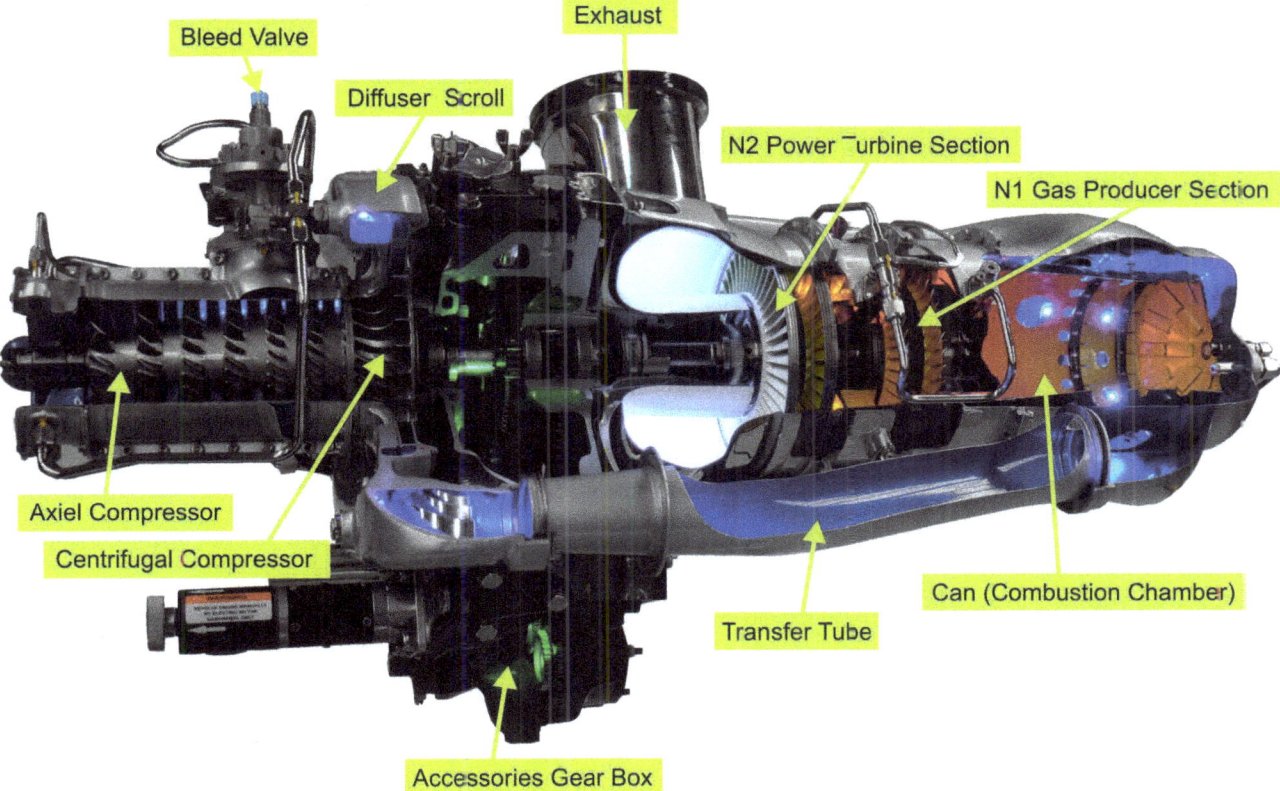

The low-pressure turbine that powers the axial and centrifugal compressors, and the high-pressure power turbines that run independently (or free) and by a concentric drive shaft (meaning two drive shafts working inside each other but independently) powers the accessories gearbox and thence the rotor system.

Gas producer turbine section

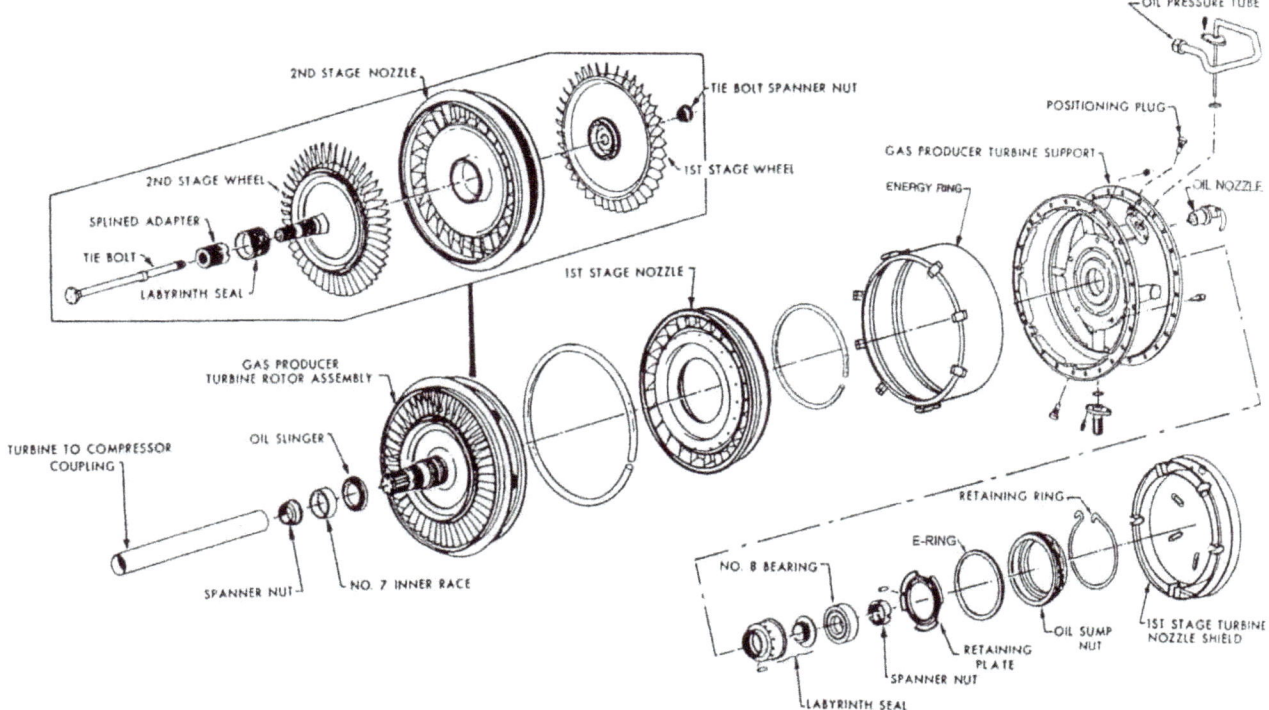

Power turbine section

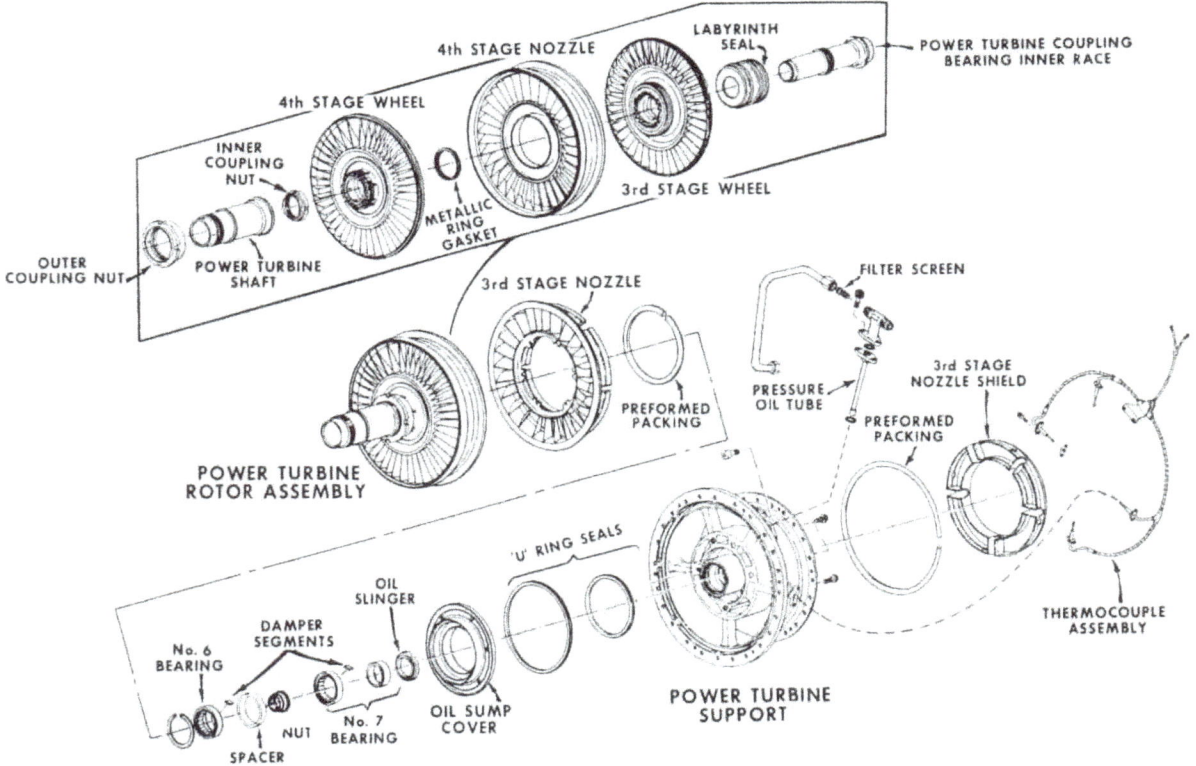

Nozzle Guide Vanes (NGVs)

The turbine nozzle guide vanes are a set of aerofoil shaped blades set in a ring and located in the turbine case. They direct the gas flow at the appropriate angle onto the first set of rotating turbine blades. Nozzle guide vanes create expansion and acceleration of the gases. Because they are not rotating, they are not subject to centrifugal forces and can have better profiles (angles) when compared to the rotating blades. The first nozzle guide vane will however be the first turbine section after the combustion chamber and will be subject to high temperatures, which makes them the most critical part of the turbine engine in terms of temperature limits. If the pilot experiences a hot start, the first nozzle guide vane is the most likely part that will initially suffer damage.

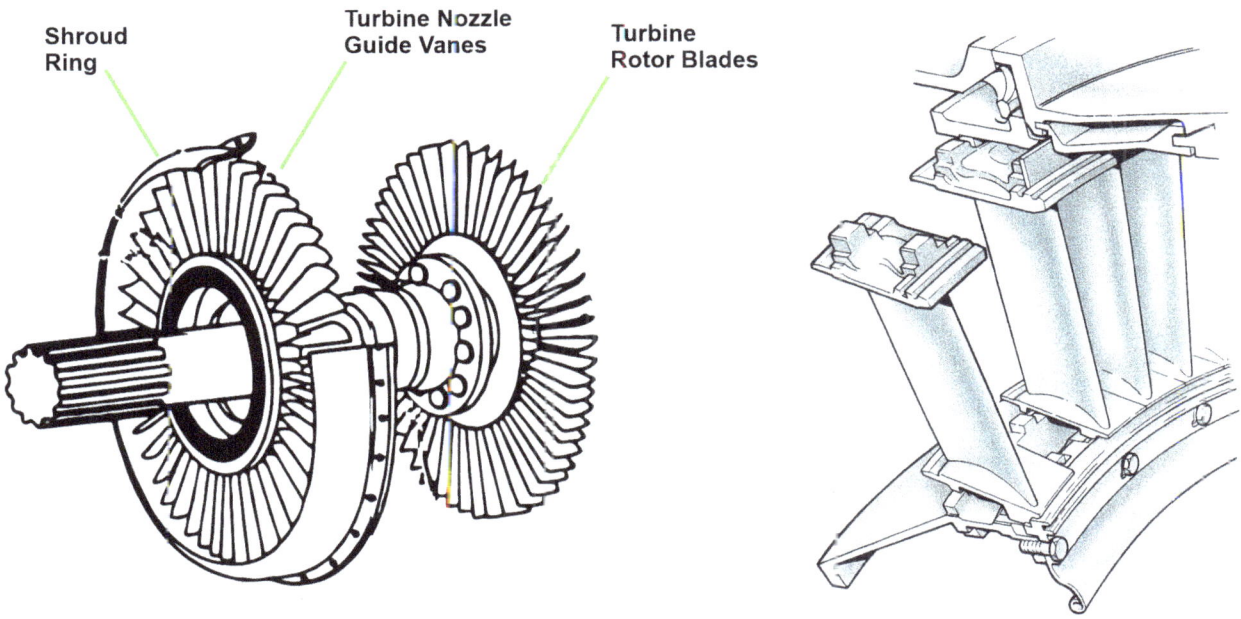

Rotating Turbine

The turbine blades are individually attached to rotating discs or wheels which are in turn attached to one of the drive shafts that transmit power to either the compressor or the accessories gearbox. Once the hot gases leave the first nozzle guide vane they act on the turbines to rotate the first turbine wheel, thus producing rotary or turbine motion. If there is more than one turbine stage, then each stage will go through the same process, extracting energy and transmitting this to a driveshaft in the process.

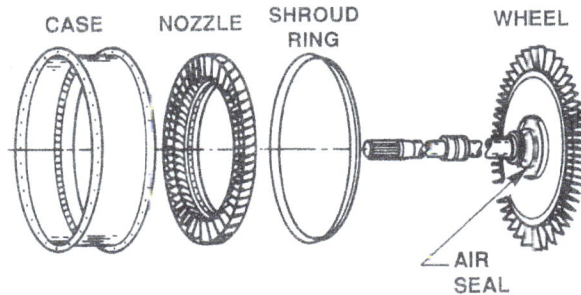

The turbine blades must be able to withstand high centrifugal forces, aerodynamic twisting and bending as well as high-temperature stresses including thermal shock (the very rapid heating and cooling of a component). Additionally, they must be resistant to oxidation, corrosion and fatigue brought on by high-frequency gas flow fluctuations, and must, therefore, be well designed and made of a material that can handle these conditions.

Turbine Blade Types

The pressure and velocity gradients through a turbine section will depend on the type or design of the fixed and rotating aerofoils. The designer's objective is to create a pair of fixed and rotating blades that achieve a significant pressure drop and velocity increase. The gas flow will have to experience a large angle of deflection and at the same time undergo expansion from low velocities to high velocities.

There are two turbine blade designs in common use. They are the impulse turbine blade and the reaction turbine blade. Together they produce the impulse-reaction design of the turbine blade.

Impulse turbine blade

The impulse blade receives the gas flow from the nozzle guide vanes (NGV), the cross-sectional area between each of the NGVs is convergent. This results in a reduction in pressure and an increase in velocity of the gas exiting the NGV. This high-velocity gas then enters a constant cross-sectional area between the impulse blades which results in a change of flow direction with little pressure or speed change. Impulse blades, therefore, receive a force provided by the impact of the gas causing the turbine wheel to turn. For impulse blades to work well, the blades need to be almost symmetrical.

To better imagine the principle of impulse blading, consider directing a water hose at a bicycle wheel. As the water hits the wheel at an angle the wheel may start to turn. It is the impact of the water onto the wheel that gives it rotation.

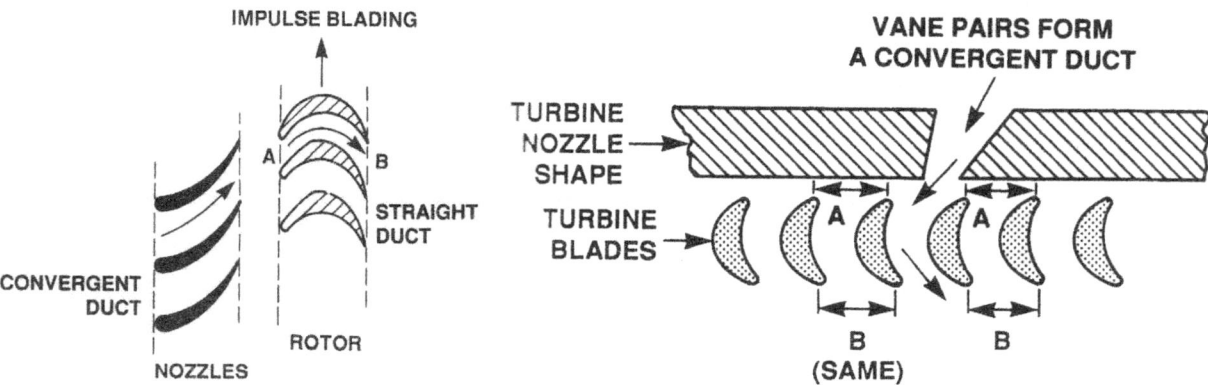

Reaction turbine blade

The reaction blade receives the gas flow from the nozzle guide vanes, the cross-sectional area between each of the NGVs remains constant but as the gas flow passes through the reaction blades, a reduction in pressure and an increase in velocity is achieved by creating a convergent duct between each of the blades giving an increase in velocity. This acceleration of the gases creates a force in the same fashion as an aerofoil; therefore the turbine disc rotates in the opposite direction to the gases leaving the turbine blades.

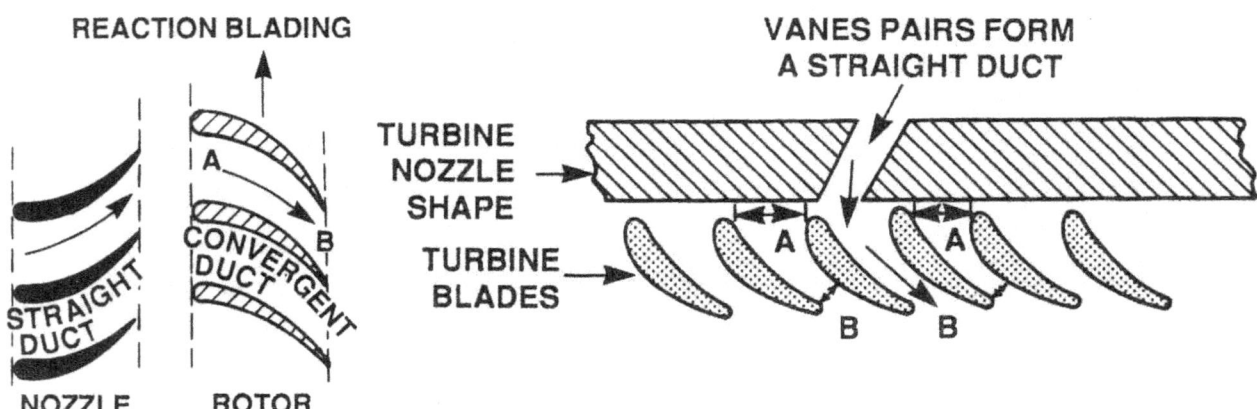

Combined effect

Although there are two basic designs of turbine blades, they are not used in their purest form due to the rotational velocity differences from the root of the blade to the tip. Instead, a combination of the impulse–reaction principles are applied along the length of the turbine blade, this necessitates a twist in the blade from root to tip which also alters the profile through the ducts between the blades from impulse blading to reaction blading.

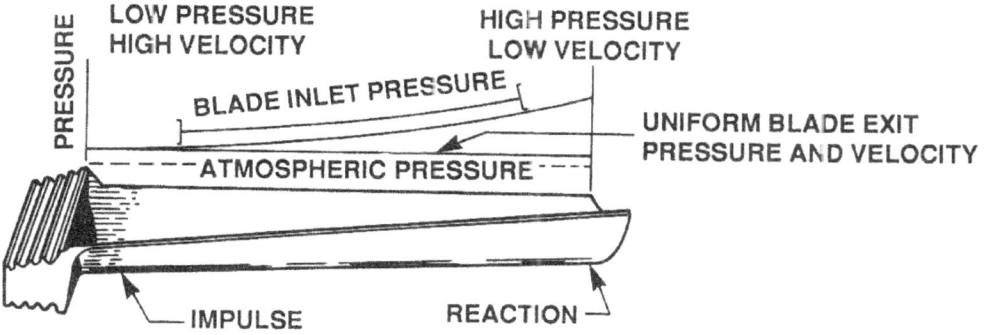

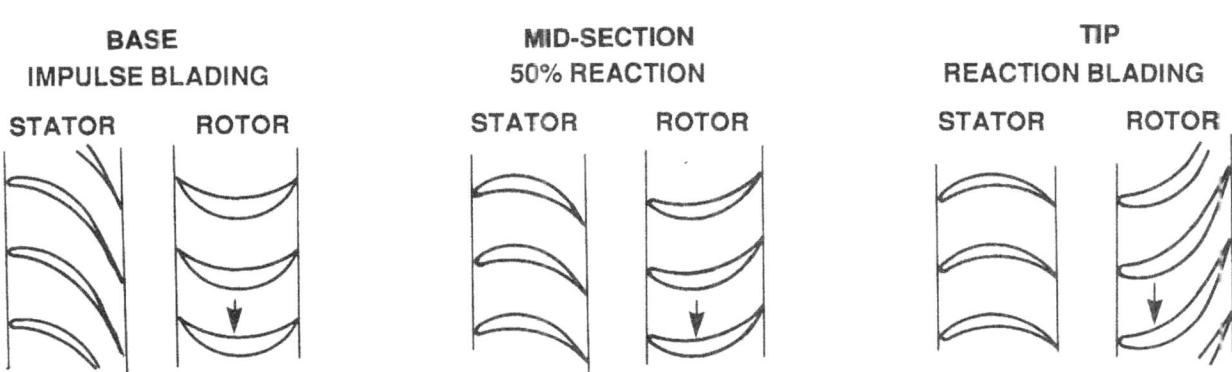

Forces on a Turbine Blade

A turbine operates by converting heat energy into mechanical energy. This process cannot be 100% efficient. Thermodynamic and mechanical losses allow approximately only 90% turbine efficiency to be achieved.

For efficient operation, the tips of the turbine blades may reach speeds of up to 1500 feet per second producing very high stresses in the rotating parts of the engine.

It has been estimated that at high rotational velocities, a single small turbine blade weighing only 2 ounces will produce a centrifugal load on the turbine rotor disc of over 2 tons, this is while turning at high speed and being exposed to temperatures of 1500°C and gas velocities of 2500 feet per second.

Blade shrouds

A design feature to reduce efficiency losses associated with gas leakage around the tips and permit a thinner blade section is to fit shrouds to the turbine blade tips.

Blade attachment

There are several different methods used to attach turbine blades to the turbine disc. When the turbine is cold, there is approximately 500ths of an inch of movement at the blade tip which is provided for at the blade root attachment point. You may have heard a 'rattle' coming from a turbine engine when it is shut down on the ground and wind is turning the turbine over. This rattle is the play in the turbine blades when cold.

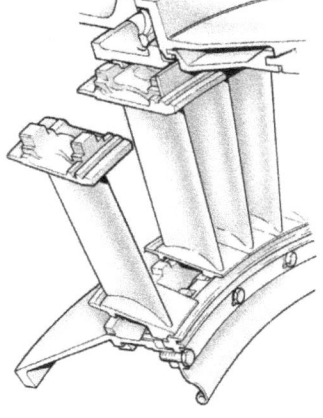

Figure 13 Turbine blade shroud

At working temperatures, the thermal expansion of the metal parts tightens the fit of the blade root onto the disc. Blades are prevented from sliding out of the disc by grooves in the side plates or by pins inserted at an angle through blade roots and discs.

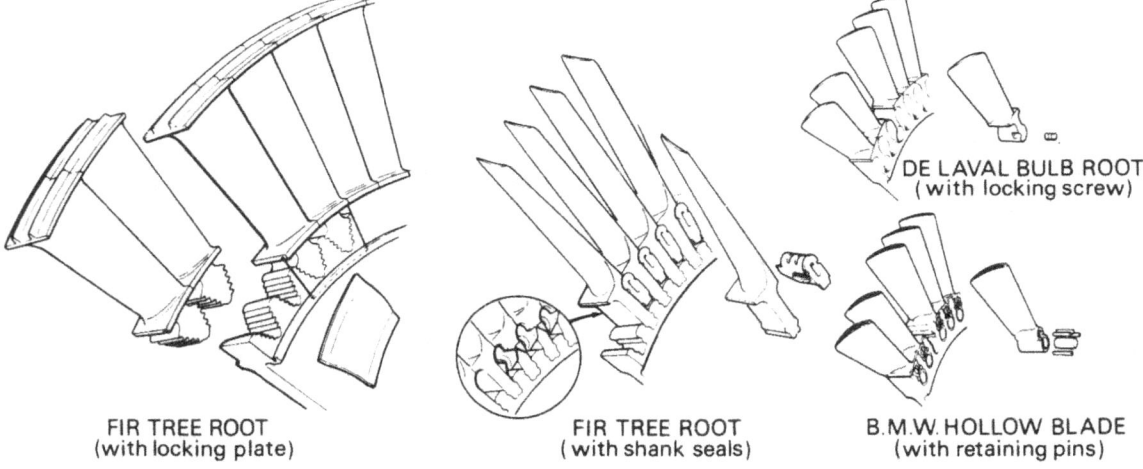

Figure 14 Turbine blade attachments

Turbine blade materials

It has been found that due to the high stresses and thermal changes a turbine blade goes through, it must be built stronger and thicker when compared to a compressor blade. The optimal aerodynamic shaping characteristics, typically with a thicker leading edge and a thin trailing edge, in a turbine blade, lead to trailing edge cracking to thermal shock at start-up and shut down.

Design and material advances have produced turbine blades that give strength, light weight, and thermal resistance. Materials including titanium, chromium and cobalt have been used in the past, and are still used now, however, advances in ceramics have led to these materials being given an additional coating of a ceramic material which improves their heat resistance and the engine's efficiency while reducing the amount of air required for cooling. Nozzle guide vanes, because they do not come under the same rotational stresses as the turbine blade often use nickel alloy in their manufacture, additionally the nozzle guide vanes use cooling air from the compressor.

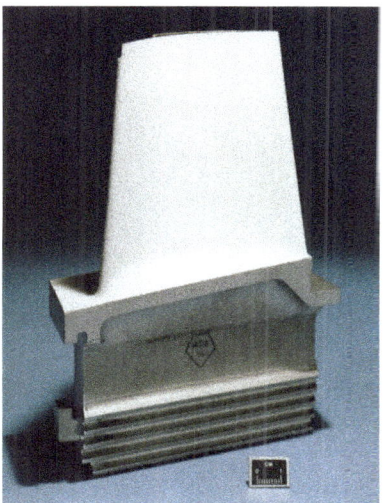

Figure 15 Turbine blade with a thermal barrier coating [10]

Turbine creep

Turbine blade creep describes the gradual and permanent elongation or 'stretching' of the turbine blades due to the combinations of centrifugal stress and temperature and the length of exposure time to these influences.

There are three turbine creep stages:

- The primary creep stage occurs during manufacture. Large changes in the material occur over a short period of time when subjected to high loads and temperatures.
- The secondary creep stage occurs over the life of the blade when in service. The manufacturer will use materials that remain safely within the relatively stable secondary creep stage. Since this area is defined by engine operating hours, it is very important that engine speed (RPM and therefore centrifugal force) and engine temperatures, particularly at the thermal shock stages of engine start and stop, are maintained within the manufacturer's limitations. Manufactures will set a limit on the number of temperature cycles certain parts of the engine may be subjected to. This is often a start and stop cycle as this is when most of the damage is done. These cycles are counted and recorded for maintenance purposes. Excursions into engine over-speeds and over-temps will lead to the blade experiencing tertiary creep.
- The tertiary creep stage is a relatively short stage where the turbine blade will progress to eventual failure.

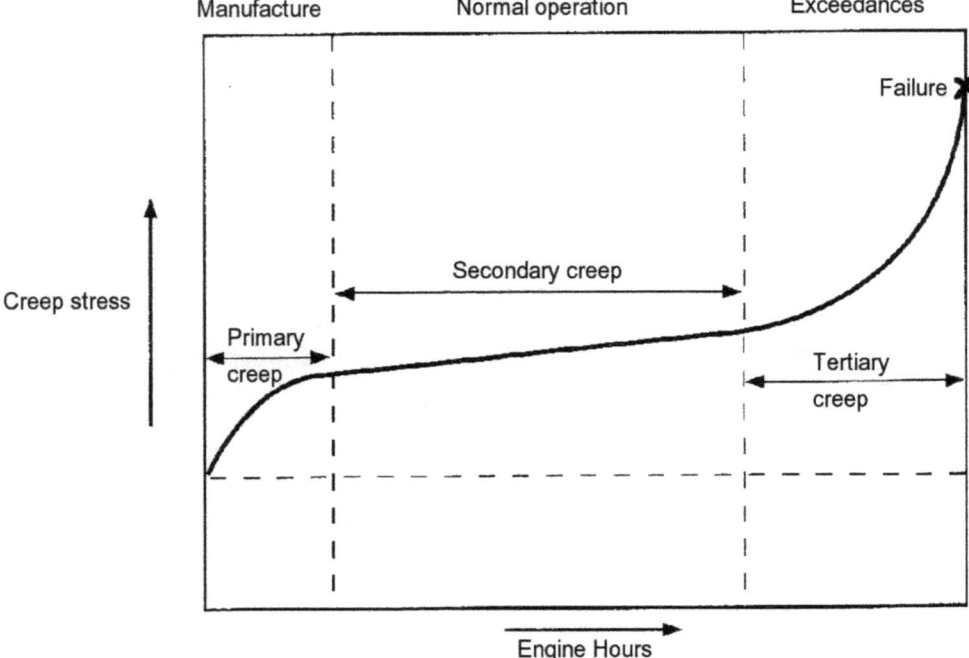

Figure 16 Turbine Creep graph

Cooling of the Turbine Section

High thermal efficiency is required in a turbine engine, and this requires high entry temperatures onto the turbine wheels. The maximum temperature will be determined by the materials that make up the turbine nozzle guide vanes. If the nozzle guide vanes were to receive some form of cooling, then the temperatures of the gas stream could actually exceed the temperature limits of the materials used to make the NGVs. This would increase engine efficiency purely by good design.

Conduction of heat from the turbine blades to the turbine disc also requires that the discs be cooled to prevent fatigue and uncontrolled expansion and contraction rates.

Air from the compressor is plumbed and directed to pass over and/or through surfaces of the turbine blades and nozzle guide vanes. There are three methods generally used, they are:

Internal air flow cooling

This is where air flows through hollow blades and vanes where the heat is carried away directly by the cooling air. This is often referred to as convection cooling.

Surface film cooling

This is where air flows from small exit ports in the leading and/or trailing edges of the vanes or blades to form a heat barrier on the surfaces.

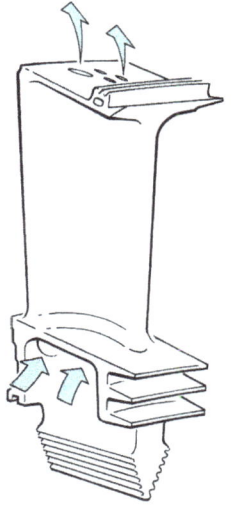

Figure 17 Internal air flow cooling

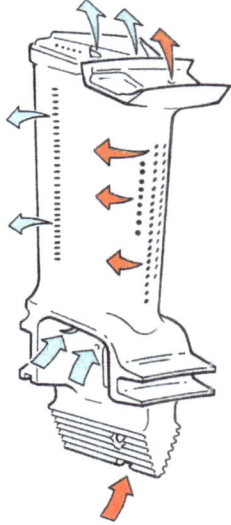

Figure 18 Surface film cooling

Combination convection and surface cooling

This is where cooling air is extracted from the gas path at the compressor section and, after cooling has been accomplished, the air is directed back into the gas path at the cooling location. The cooling air is relative as it may still be several hundred degrees Celsius, the important thing to remember is it is relatively cooler than the surface and the surrounding air it is trying to cool.

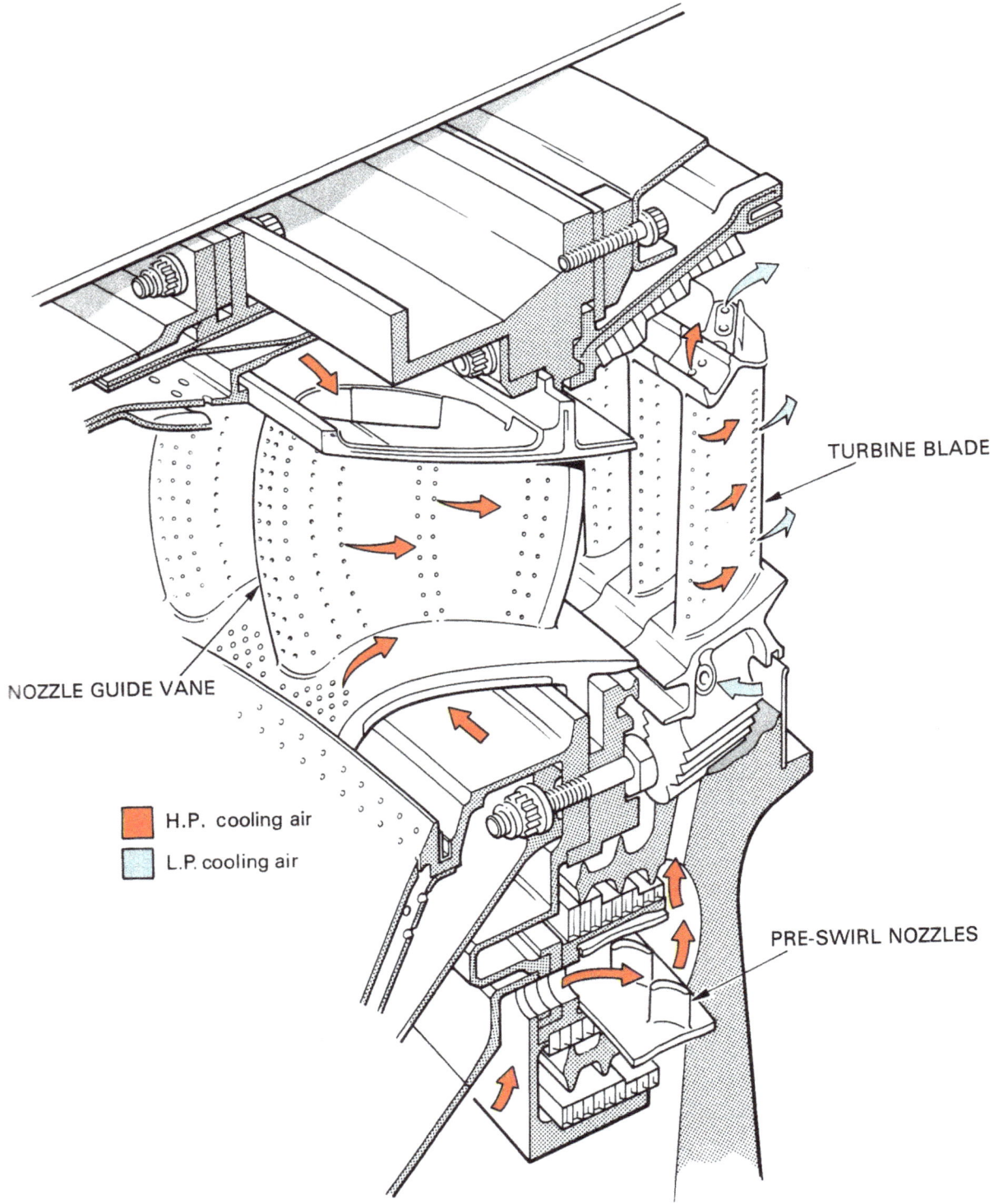

Accessory Drive Section

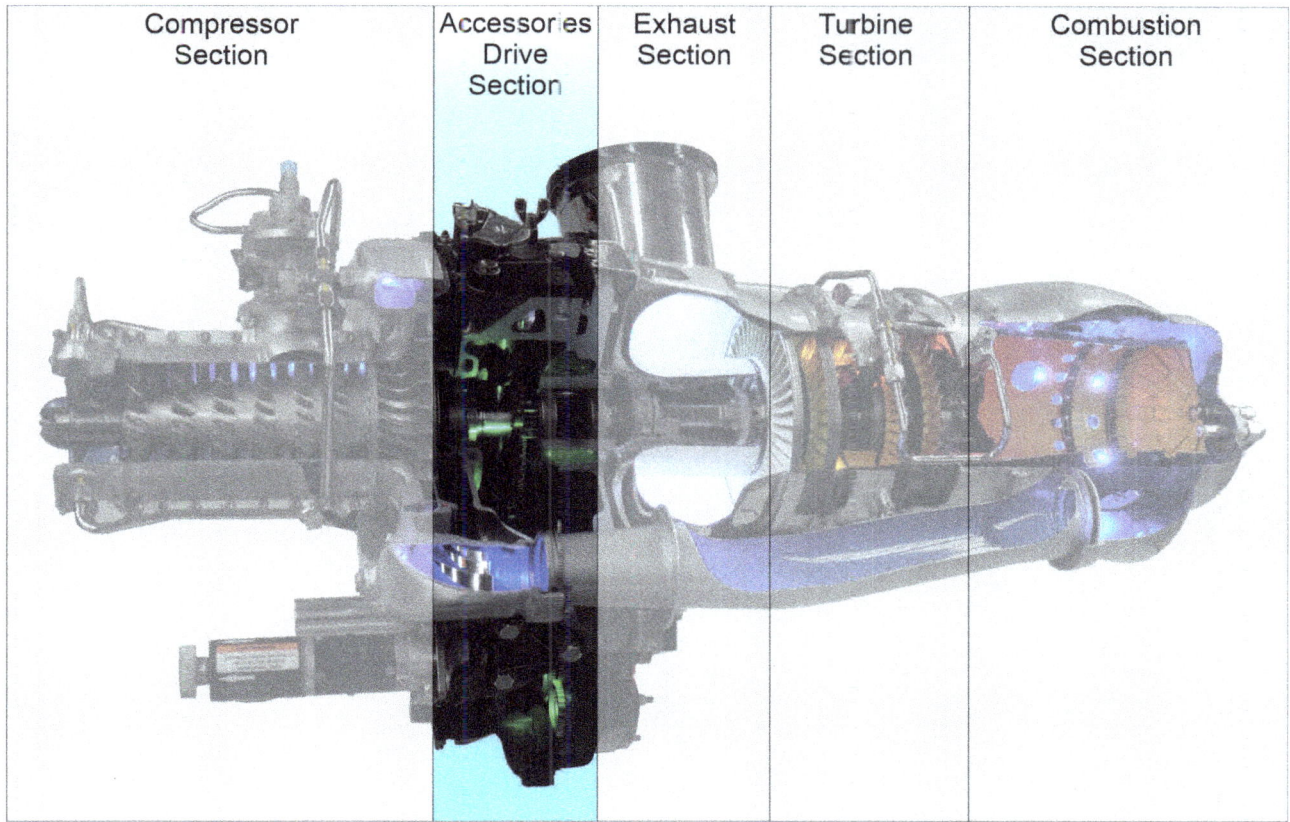

Accessory gearboxes come in various design shapes and configurations, the result is the accessory units that provide power for the aircraft, including the hydraulic, pneumatic and electrical systems as well as various pumps (fuel and oil) and control systems for efficient engine operation must somehow be powered or driven.

Ultimately these accessories are powered by a driveshaft coming from either the gas producer or the power turbine driveshaft which in turn will rotate other intermeshing gears which in turn drive or rotate the accessory units.

For fire safety reasons most accessories are grouped around the cold section of the engine and are attached directly to the gearbox on faced pads.

In turboshaft engines used in helicopters the combined power and accessory gearbox is the primary structural member of the engine because it provides mounting and support for the compressor and turbine assemblies.

The accessory gearbox contains most of the lubrication system components and incorporates two separate gear trains.

In the Rolls Royce C250C20 engine the power turbine gear train reduces power turbine speed from approximately 34000 engine RPM to approximately 6100 RPM giving a gear reduction of 5.53:1. The accessories gearbox then has an output shaft into the main rotor transmission where it is further reduced so that the rotor blades turn at approximately 400 RPM.

The power turbine gear train also incorporates the torque meter assembly and drives the power turbine tachometer generator and the power turbine governor.

The gas producer gear train drives the oil pump, the fuel pump, gas producer fuel control, the gas producer tachometer gearbox and the starter generator.

During starting, the starter generator cranks the engine through the gas producer gear train, rotating the compressor to draw air into the combustion chamber.

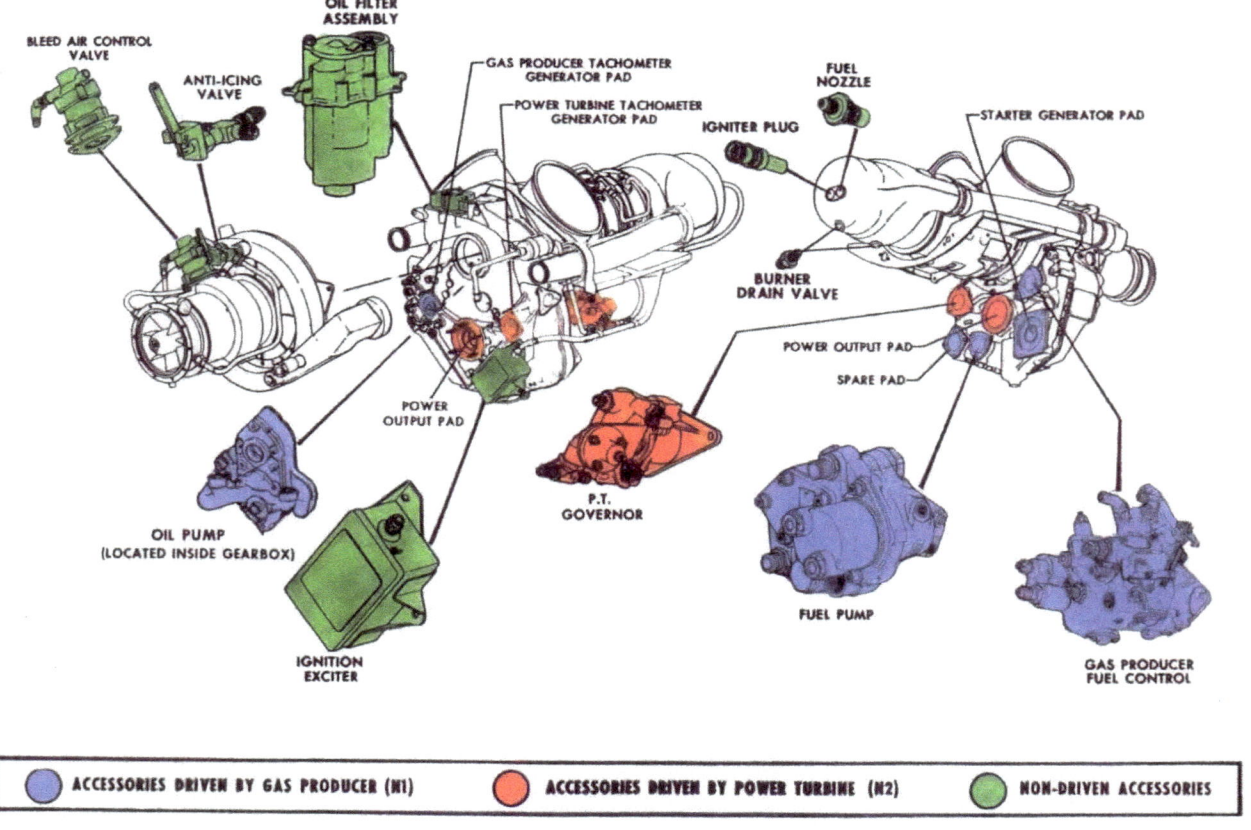

The gearbox housing and cover are magnesium-alloy castings. They house bearings used to support the power turbine and gas producer gear trains. Magnesium alloy is used because it is very light, however, a big disadvantage of magnesium alloy is it is highly flammable therefore any fire in the engine bay must be dealt with immediately.

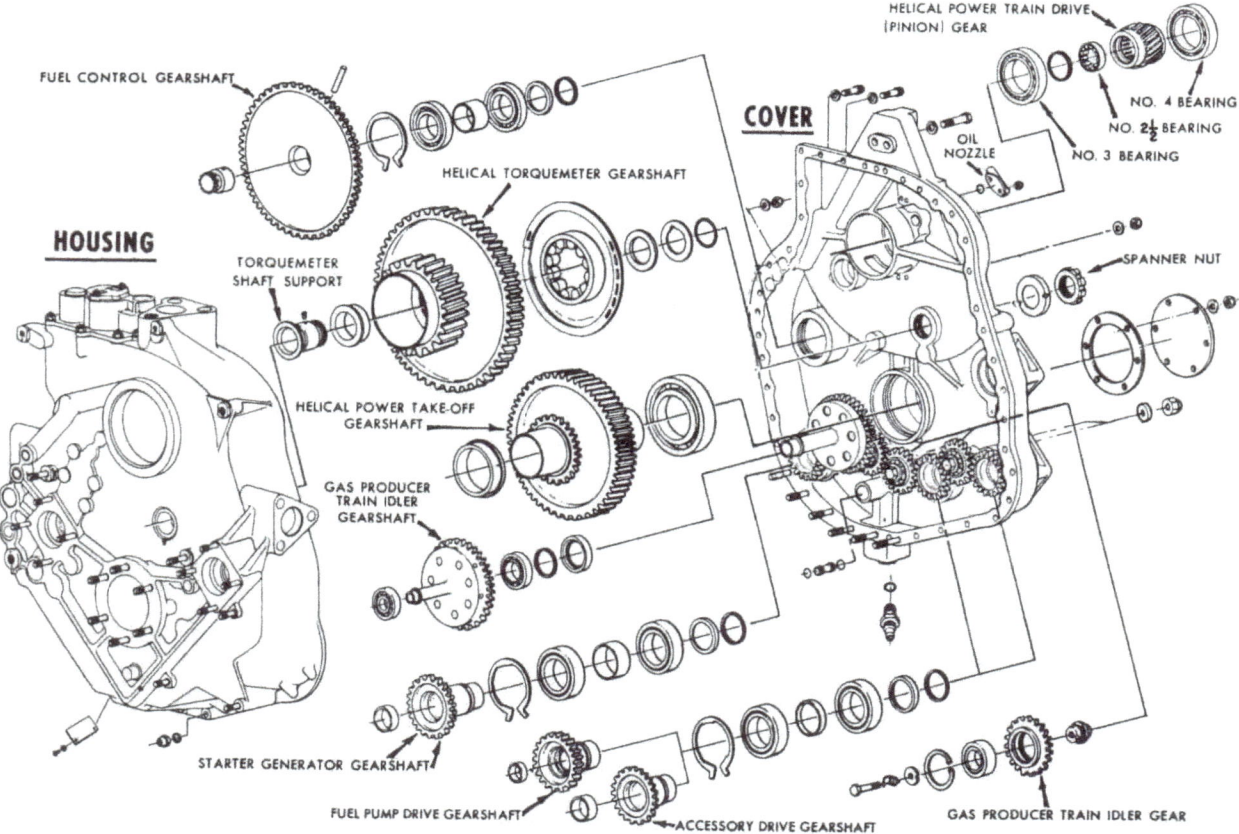

Exhaust Section

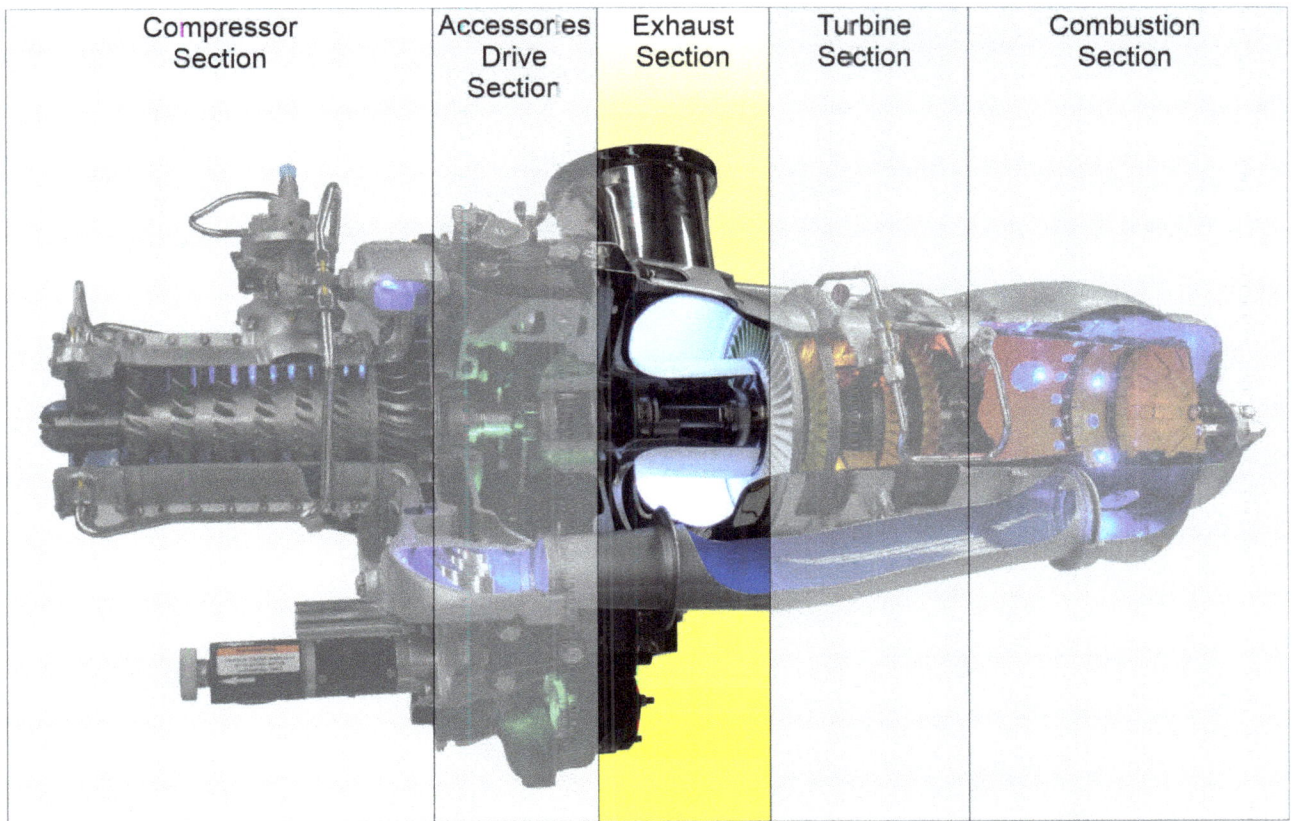

Turbo jet engines have an exhaust system that passes the gases from the turbine to the atmosphere at a velocity and a direction to give thrust. In a turboshaft engine or a turboprop, only a small amount of thrust is given by the exhaust duct. Most of the energy is used by the turbine for driving the gearbox and compressor.

In a helicopter, the exhaust provides no thrust but must be designed to aid turbine efficiency as well as direct the exhaust gases away from the helicopter's airframe. This is most obvious at the hover where the exhaust gases may be directed to the tail boom where the excess heat may in time cause fatiguing.

The temperature of gases entering the exhaust system can be between 550 and 850 degrees (if an afterburner is fitted then the temperature can be over 1500 degrees) so appropriate materials are required for construction to withstand cracking and distortion.

Below is a photo of a Squirrel that has been doing prolonged periods of sling work at the hover. Note the black burn marks from the exhaust gases.

Gas Flow

Gas will enter the exhaust at velocities of up to 1200 feet/second. Gas velocities of this magnitude produce high friction losses, so the gas is slowed down using diffusion.

Additional losses occur due to the swirling of the airflow (this comes from the residual effect of the turbine) so the turbine rear struts in the exhaust unit are designed to straighten out the airflow before passage into the exhaust pipe.

In fixed-wing, the exhaust pipe or 'jet' pipe carries the airflow to the propelling nozzle. This is a convergent duct designed to increase the velocity of airflow to provide extra thrust in a turbo jet engine.

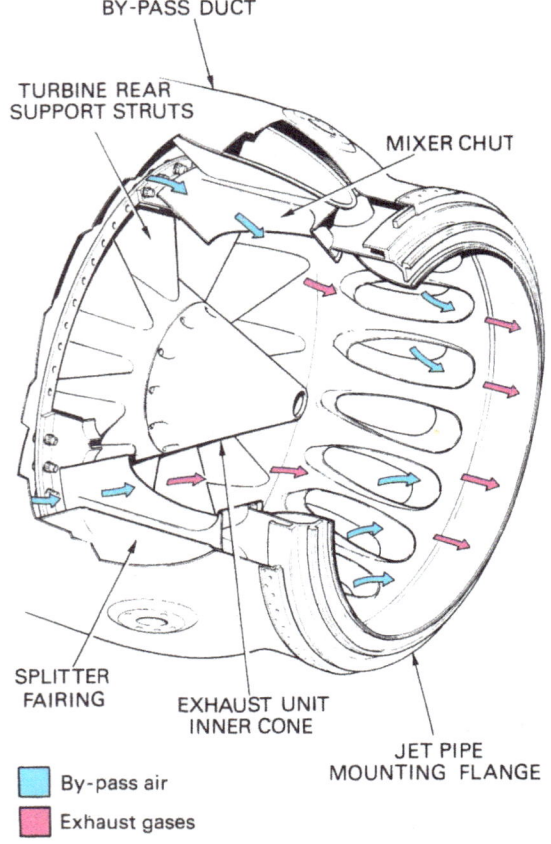

Noise Suppression

There are two methods to reduce noise levels used by engine manufacturers, they are:

- Using sound-absorbent materials.
- Designing to minimise noise produced and bringing about rapid dispersal of that noise.

The noise coming from a gas turbine engine exhaust, for the most part, is low-frequency noise (like a ship's foghorn) and it carries a long way. Because of the tendency of low-frequency noise to linger at high volumes, noise reduction is achieved by raising the frequency of the sound. This frequency change is achieved by increasing the perimeter or size of the exhaust stream, which allows more room for hot and cold gas mixing. More room stops the hot and cold air molecules from rubbing or shearing against each other. It also breaks up the large turbulence in the jet wake that produces low-frequency noise. In other words, reducing the large eddy turbulence to fine-grain turbulence changes the frequency of noise to a higher state which is more readily absorbed by the atmosphere.

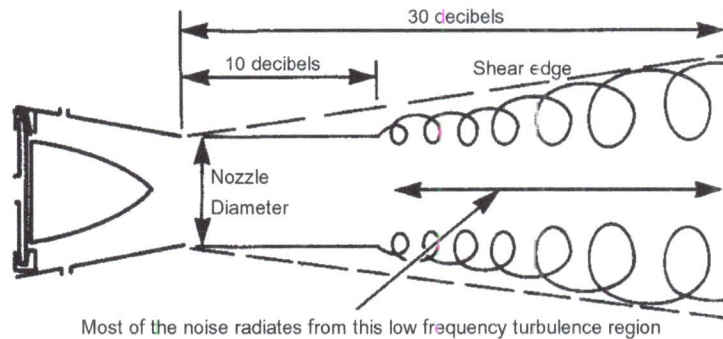

Most of the noise radiates from this low frequency turbulence region

Levels in Decibels

Below is a brief list of common noises and their decibel level.

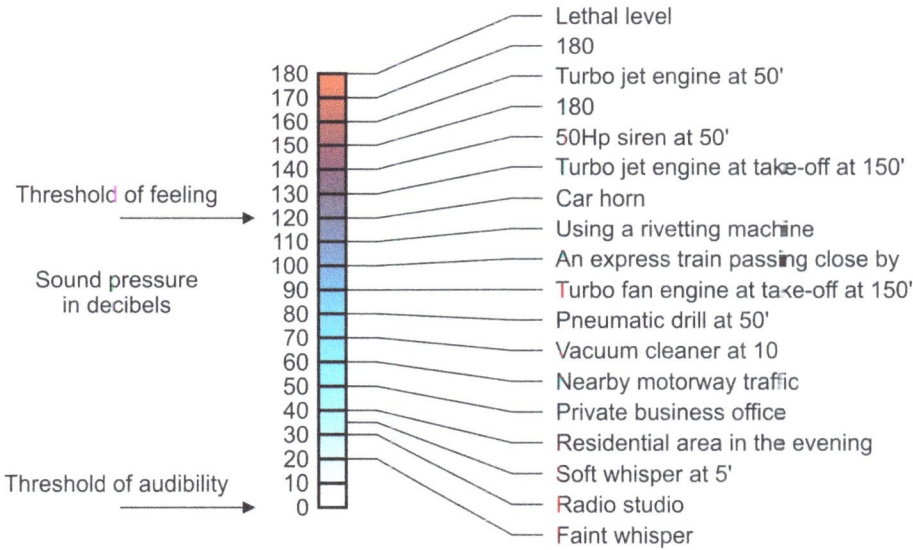

Noise suppression in helicopters

In helicopters, noise generated by the turbine is often secondary to the noise generated by the tail rotor and main rotor blades. For this reason, turbine exhausts are usually very simple and are designed more to encourage the efficient flow of gas promoting better engine efficiency as well as directing the exhaust gases away from the fuselage as previously stated. Also, the additional features of an exhaust system such as thrust augmentation (afterburners), reverse thrust and convergent-divergent nozzle theory (for supersonic aircraft) are relevant to fixed-wing aircraft only and will not be discussed here.

Mike Becker, Becker Helicopters

Fuel Control Systems in a Turbine Engine

The fuel control system in a helicopter turbine engine typically comprises of the following:

- Electric fuel boost pumps.
- Engine-driven fuel pressure pump.
- A fuel/oil heat exchanger (becoming common in European helicopters).
- Fuel filters.
- Fuel control unit (FCU).
- Governor system.
- Fuel spray nozzles and plumbing.
- Plumbing.

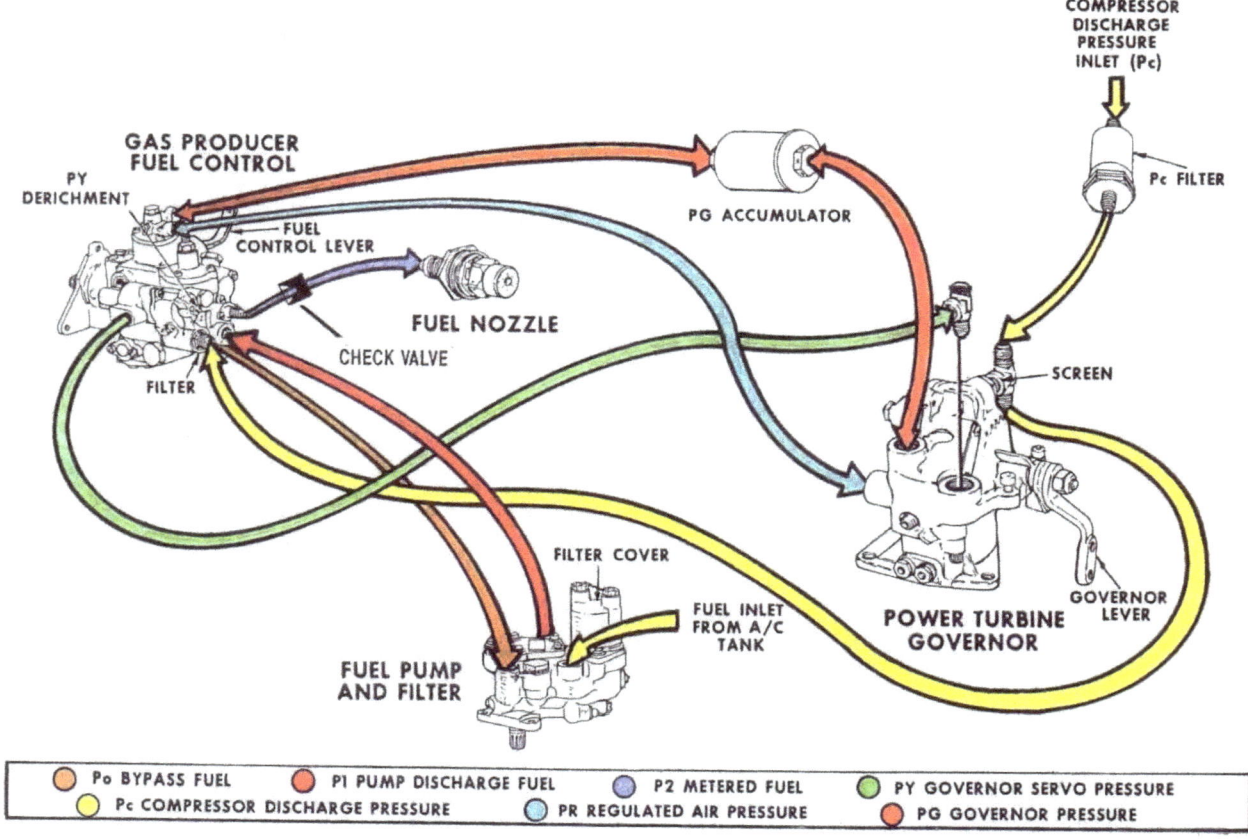

Electric Fuel Boost Pumps

Low-pressure electric fuel boost pumps are located inside the helicopter's fuel tanks and provide fuel to the high-pressure engine-driven fuel pump located on the engine. In most helicopters the fuel tank is below the engine, so a positive pressure is required under all phases of flight. The electric booster pumps are usually powerful enough to supply a sufficient fuel flow rate and pressure to enable engine operation under all flight conditions in the event of an engine-driven fuel pump failure. However, many helicopters will have limitations as the pumps become less efficient at altitude.

For example, in the Jet Ranger, both electric pumps are allowed to be inoperative if operating below 6000ft AMSL. Once above 6000ft, at least one pump must be operative.

Figure 19 Circuit breakers to activate fuel pumps

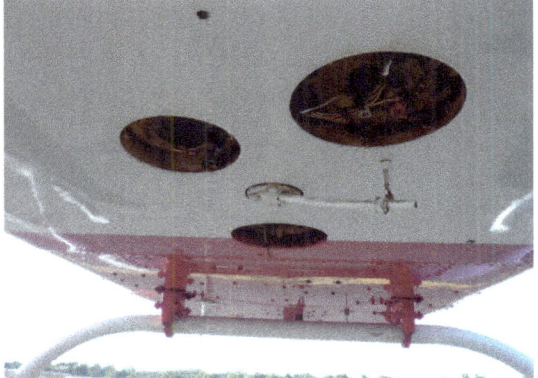

Figure 20 Pumps mounted in the fuel tank

Engine Driven Fuel Pumps

As fuel supplied by the low-pressure electric boost pumps reaches the engine-driven high-pressure pump, the pressure is boosted to several hundred psi. This makes high-pressure fuel available to the fuel control unit (FCU) which in turn meters the fuel as appropriate to the fuel nozzles and governor unit to meet the demands in the combustion chamber.

There are two basic types of engine-driven pumps; they are the positive displacement pump and the plunger pump. Below is an example of a plunger-type pump.

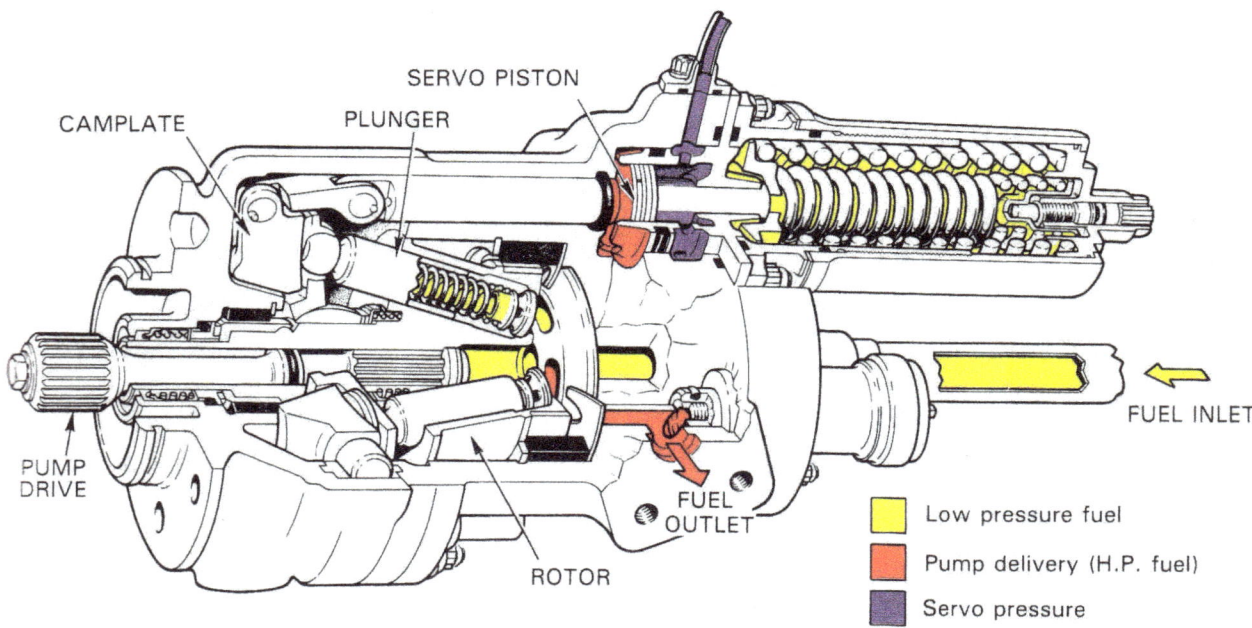

Any excess fuel delivered by the high-pressure pump will be recycled back into the fuel system by plumbing, usually upstream of the low-pressure fuel filter. The bypass process is affected by a spill valve. Sensitive to pressure drops across the metering units in the FCU system, it opens or closes to regulate excess fuel as required.

It should also be noted that the fuel itself will act as a lubricant for the engine-driven pump and associated valves in the FCU.

Fuel Control Unit (FCU) and Governors

The pilot controls power by using the collective/throttle. The throttle in a turbine is used mainly for starting and stopping and in some cases in emergencies. Once a turbine is started, the throttle is usually set to full ON and the collective therefore is the primary power lever.

Controlling the power output of the engine is achieved by varying the amount of fuel fed into the combustion chamber.

Increasing power by raising the collective produces a greater fuel flow and increases fuel pressure to the fuel nozzles in the combustion chamber. The gas temperature (TOT, TIT, ITT) increases, which in turn increases the acceleration of the gas increasing engine RPM and therefore the total gas flow.

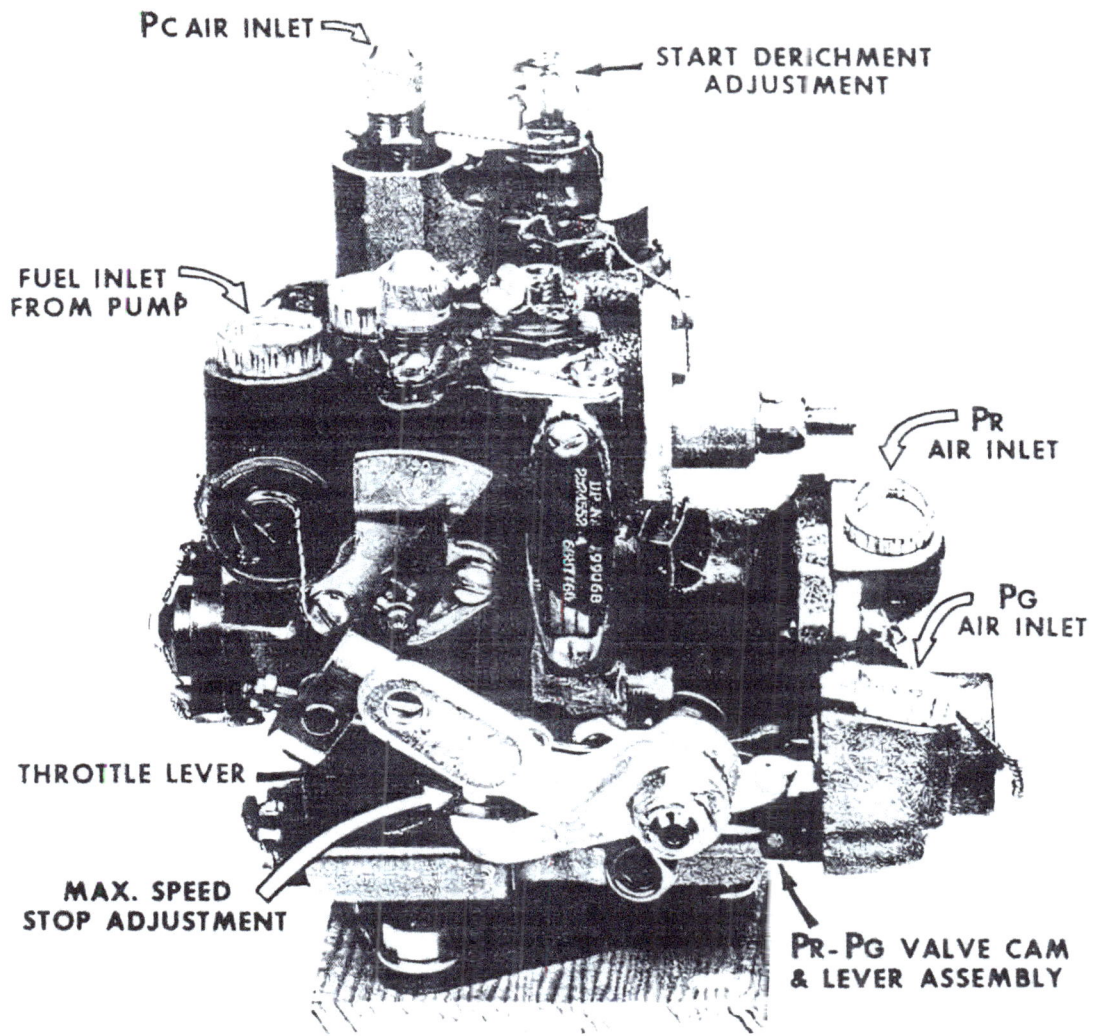

The FCU is a very complex and finely engineered device with many small holes, tubes and pressure sensors. It must compensate for the many variables that make up air density (altitude, temperature, airspeed) in controlling the power output of the engine.

Engine handling would not be possible without the interrelationships of the controlling and regulating devices and automatic operations of the FCU.

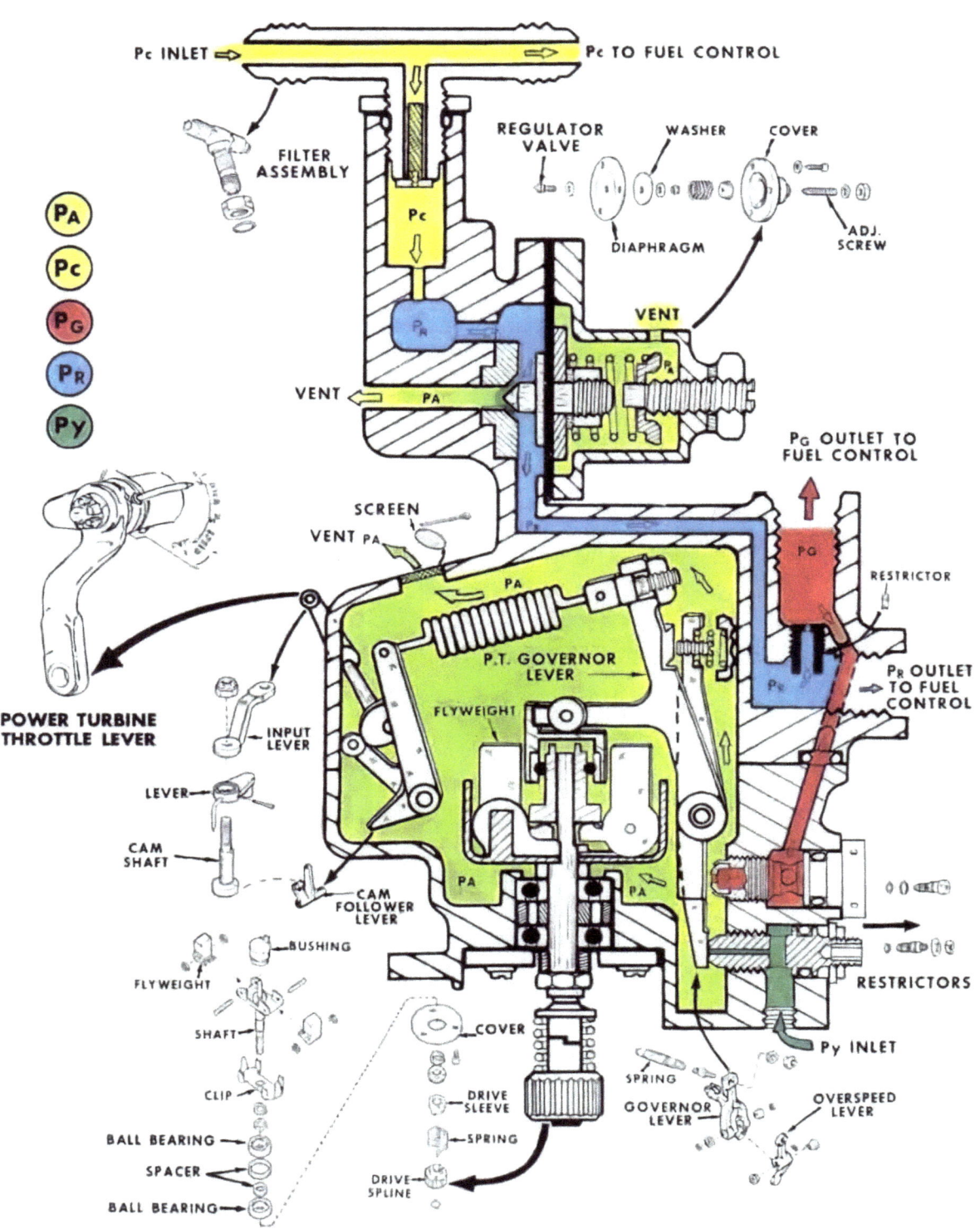

Having clean fuel is very important as any contaminants may prevent the proper functioning of the FCU.

Basic Gas Turbines *for Helicopter Pilots*

Throttle positions

In a helicopter, it is desirable for the Rotor RPM to be kept at a constant regardless of the pitch being applied by the pilot.

The throttle will have three basic positions:

- OFF. No fuel is being delivered into the combustion chamber.
- IDLE: The throttle has been wound onto the first detent position and enough fuel is directed into the combustion chamber for starting and for the turbine to run at a ground idle which is normally around 50-60% compressor speed with the Rotor RPM at 70%.
- ON: The throttle has been wound to the full ON position and enough fuel is delivered into the combustion chamber to allow the engine to run at full flight idle which is normally around 90% compressor speed with the Rotor RPM at 100%.

With the throttle set at full ON and the collective full down the turbine will be idling at flight idle.

Throttle OFF　　　　　　　**Throttle IDLE**　　　　　　　**Throttle ON**

FCU OFF　　　　　　　**FCU IDLE**　　　　　　　**FCU ON**

 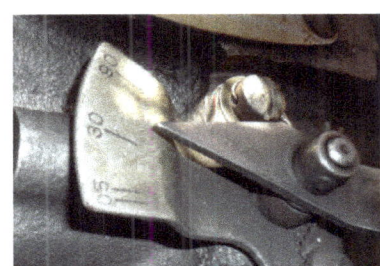 

Once the throttle is full-on, the pilot can now increase rotor pitch. Increases and decreases in rotor pitch will increase and decrease rotor drag and therefore the power required from the turbine will increase and decrease. The FCU's job is to detect these changes in power requirement and deliver more or less fuel into the combustion chamber.

Setting the throttle to full ON *allows* the FCU to use up to its maximum N1 RPM, to keep the N2 RPM at the selected setting. If the throttle is set slightly less than full, and the pilot keeps pulling the collective, the N2 and rotor RPM will eventually decay because the throttle will not allow the FCU to give the N1 enough fuel to meet the power demand.

If the collective is raised, the FCU will detect a change in fuel requirement and deliver more fuel, this will give rise to an increase in turbine temperature and an increase in the mass airflow passing through the turbine which will:

- Increase power available and therefore maintain Rotor RPM as the pitch is increased.
- Increase compressor speed which is required to deliver more air to the combustion chamber to be mixed with the increased fuel flow to give more power as being demanded by the rotor system.

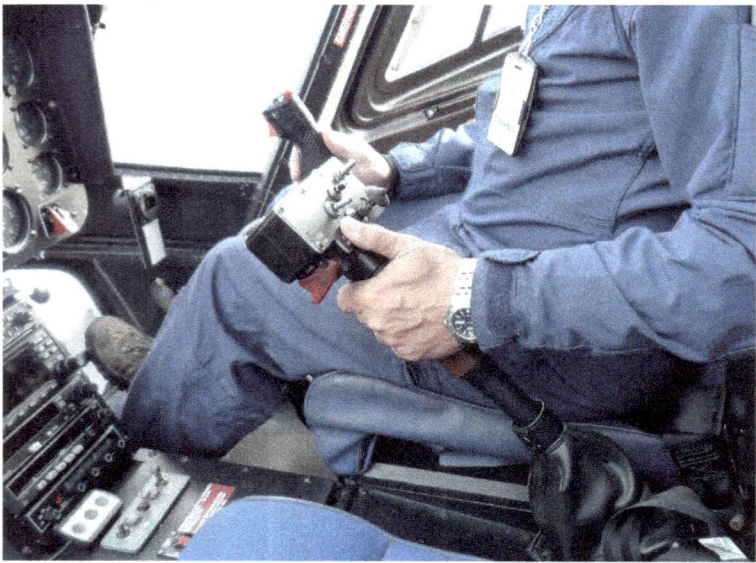

If the collective is lowered, the FCU will detect a change in fuel requirement and deliver less fuel, this will give rise to a decrease in turbine temperature and a decrease in the mass airflow passing through the turbine which will:

- Decrease power available and therefore maintain Rotor RPM as the pitch is decreased.
- Decrease compressor speed which is required to deliver less air to the combustion chamber to be mixed with the decreased fuel flow to give less power as being demanded by the rotor system.

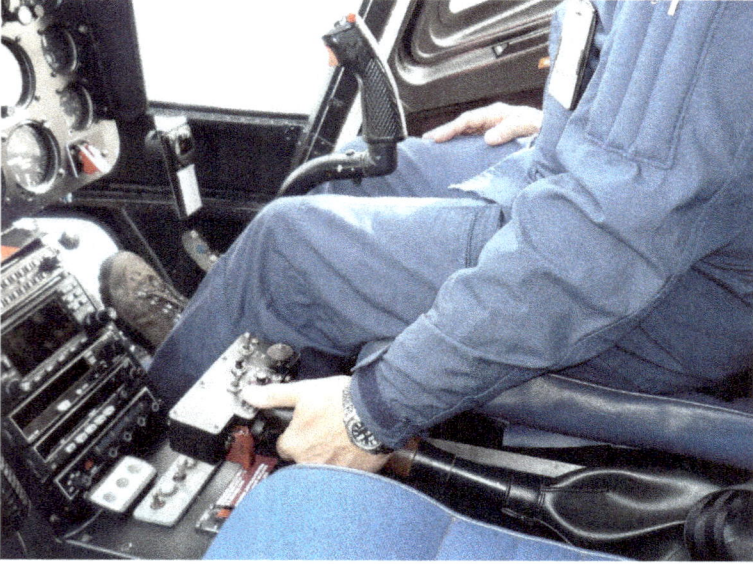

Basic Gas Turbines *for Helicopter Pilots*

Governor

When the pilot raises and lowers the collective, it will take time for the fuel control unit to detect the changes. This can lead to a lag in response and can be seen by the Rotor RPM dropping (dropping below the normal flight idle RPM) if the collective is raised or having a transient over speed (increasing above the upper RPM limit) if the collective is lowered.

To minimise this problem and control RPM, manufacturers may install one or more of the following:

- Anticipator cable
- Automatic governor
- Beep governor

The anticipator cable and automatic governor do the same thing. They are directly connected to the collective and immediately sense any movement by the pilot. This movement is transmitted either mechanically by a cable or electronically through a computer and either delivers more or less fuel as required in anticipation of the FCU following behind. This reduces the effects of the lag in the FCU.

Some governors are very accurate and work very well with pilots not being able to see any changes in RPM with movements of the collective. Some governors are not very good at all, and you will still see significant droop or over speed.

The beep governor is usually an additional device for fine-tuning the N2 and rotor RPM of the engine and the rotor. This is a coarse device that has a small range allowing the pilot to independently anticipate or 'beep' the RPM to a desired setting. It is used to counter the effects of density altitude, heavy loads or harsh manoeuvring and is a manual method of base-lining the FCU to better do its job. Not all helicopters have this additional governor.

The beep control is activated by the pilot with a switch on the collective, this, in turn, activates an electric motor and a worm drive, combined they form a device known as a linear actuator, this actuator works on the throttle lever of the N2 governor to give more or less fuel to the FCU.

B206 Collective "beep" Control

B206 Linear Actuator

Power Turbine Governor in the B206

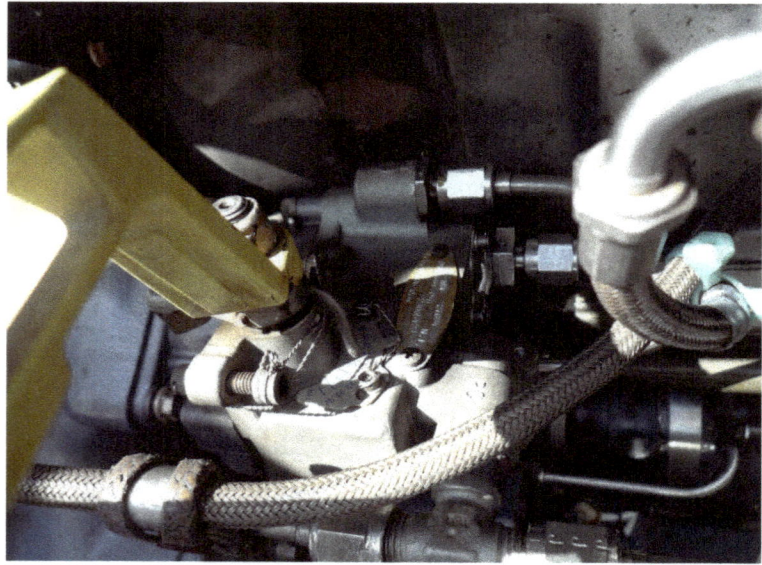

Example

In a Jet Ranger, the beep governor may be used at any time to adjust the Rotor RPM. It operates within an RPM range of 97% and 102% RRPM. Once the pilot has selected the desired RRPM the FCU will work to keep the RPM at that level. Small droops and transients will be centred around that figure.

Basic Gas Turbines *for Helicopter Pilots*

Electronic Engine Control Systems

With the advent of computers, many new helicopters are being delivered with electronic engine control systems.

This includes some of the following terms and definitions: EEC, FFR, FMU, FADEC, FAFC, DAU.

Electronic Engine Control (EEC)

The Electronic Engine Control (EEC) is designed to monitor engine performance and make necessary control inputs to maintain certain engine parameters (temperature, RPM of the compressor and turbine, torque values) within predetermined limits.

Fuel Flow Regulator (FFR)

The Fuel Flow Regulator (FFR) and Fuel Metering Unit (FMU) receive information from the EEC. The FFR and FMU can regulate the amount of fuel going into the combustion chamber. Often these units are used as limiters. If the EEC detects an RPM or a temperature that is going to exceed a limit then a message is sent to the FFR or FMU to reduce the fuel flow and therefore automatically protect the engine from damage.

Full Authority Digital Engine Control (FADEC)

The Full Authority Digital Engine Control (FADEC) electronically controls all of the engine parameters. It replaces the traditional FCU with its many hydro-mechanical and air pressure elements with a computer. The pilot is therefore required to do less of the engine management, with the fuel system consisting only of a fuel pump, some form of fuel metering and an independent fuel shutoff valve in case of a computer (FADEC) failure.

The FADEC will start, continuously run and shut down the engine by command of the pilot. The pilot cannot directly influence the FADECs management of the engine.

Full Authority Fuel Control (FAFC)

The Full Authority Fuel Control (FAFC) provides full electronic control of the engine fuel system only. Unlike the FADEC it does not have the transient control intelligence to control the compressor speed.

Data Acquisition Unit (DAU)

The Data Acquisition Unit (DAU) is a computer that collects all the information from the various helicopter systems and then either displays this to the pilot on an electronic display unit (EDU) sometimes referred to as the IDS or Integrated Display system. The DAU may also send this information to the EEC, the FADEC or FAFC.

Below is an Agusta 109E DAU and the EDU it displays on.

Figure 21 Agusta 109E DAU

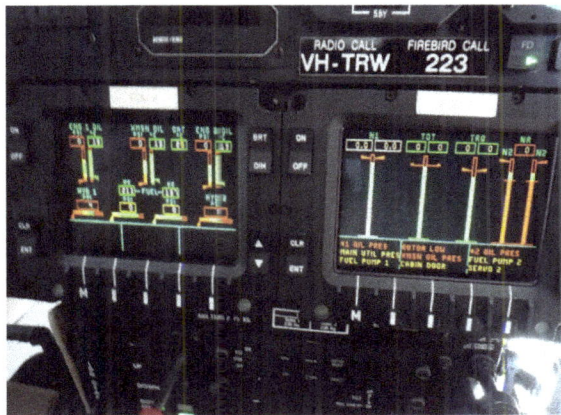

Figure 22 Agusta 109E EDU

Fuel Spray Nozzles

Helicopter turbines typically have one or more fuel spray nozzles which have the job of atomising the fuel into a fine spray as it enters the combustion chamber to ensure its rapid and even burning.

This is quite a difficult task due to the velocity of the airflow coming from the compressor and the short time available to complete the burning process due to the velocity of the gases.

Fuel vaporisation is achieved by passing fuel through swirl chambers. These are tangentially (opposing angles) arranged orifices (holes) that impart a swirl to the fuel particles which emerge as a cone of fuel spray.

When ignited this gives the flame in the combustion chamber the right shape.

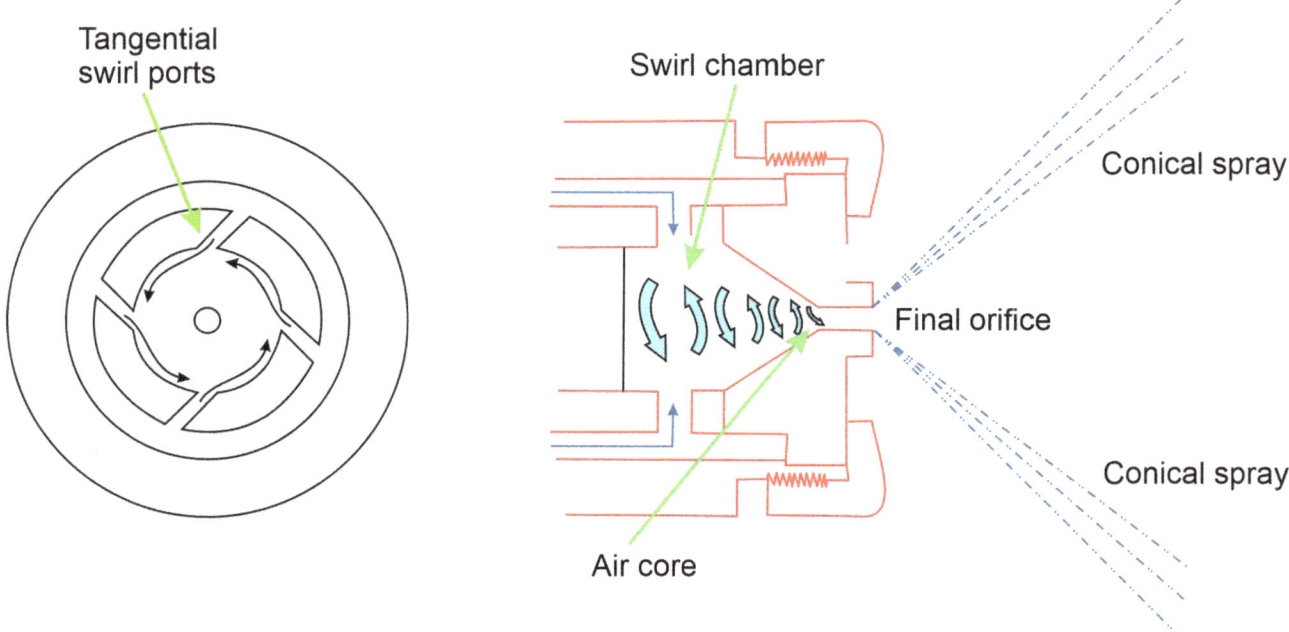

Obviously, if the fuel nozzle becomes damaged or dirty then the fuel spray pattern will not be efficient enough to promote good combustion and engine efficiency will be lost. In the worst-case scenario the flame will extinguish (flame out) and the engine will stop.

One of the common areas of contamination is at installation if an engineer happens to put a dirty finger on the outlet of the nozzle, this alone can disrupt the perfect spray.

The fuel spray pattern may vary depending on RPM and fuel flow pressures.

At low fuel pressures, a continuous film of fuel is formed known as a bubble.

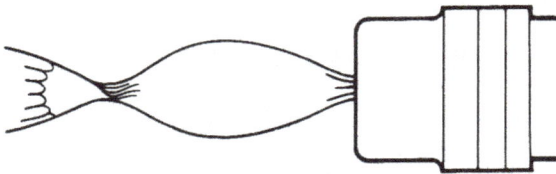

At intermediate fuel pressures, the film breaks up at the edges to form a 'tulip'.

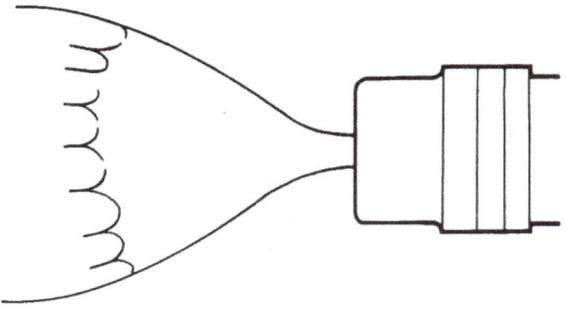

At high fuel pressures, the tulip shortens towards the orifice and forms a finely atomised spray.

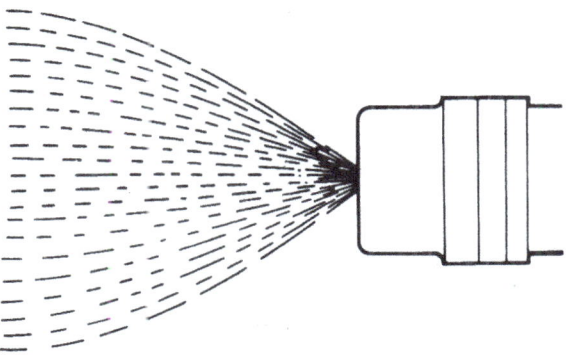

There are two types of fuel nozzle. They are the simplex and the duplex spray nozzle.

Simplex

The simplex fuel nozzle is a pressure jet atomiser with a single fuel manifold. It incorporates a swirl into the fuel and a fixed area atomising nozzle. The simplex spray nozzle works well at high flow rates but at lower rates, the shape of the spray cone is inadequate for efficient burning.

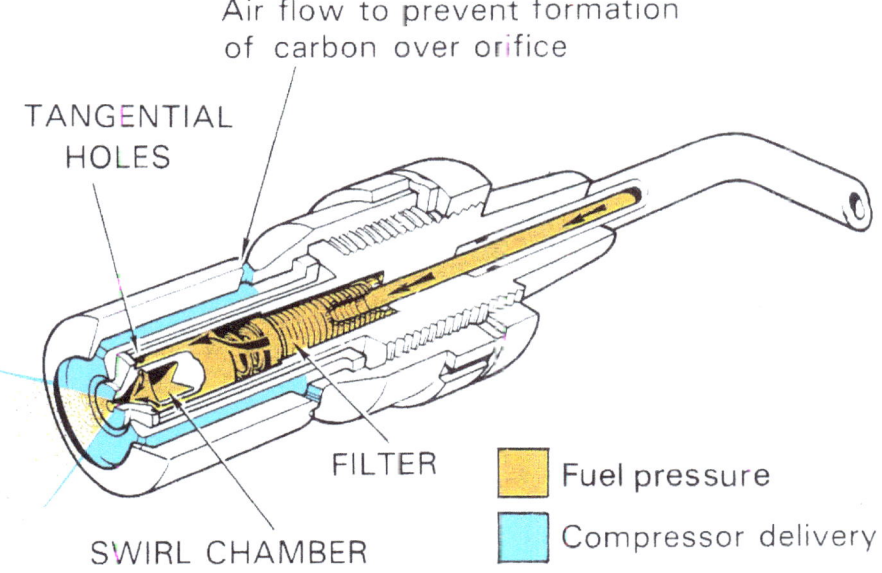

Duplex

The duplex fuel nozzle requires a primary and a secondary fuel feed manifold and has two independent orifices, one larger than the other.

A pressurising valve is used to apportion the fuel to each of the manifolds at the appropriate time. The primary manifold has a smaller orifice and provides fuel for the lower rate of flow required at lower power settings. As power is increased and therefore fuel flow and pressure increase, the pressurising valves move to progressively admit fuel to the secondary or main manifold with its larger orifice. This will give a combined flow through both manifolds allowing an even burning when large quantities of fuel are required.

Helicopters typically have a duplex fuel nozzle.

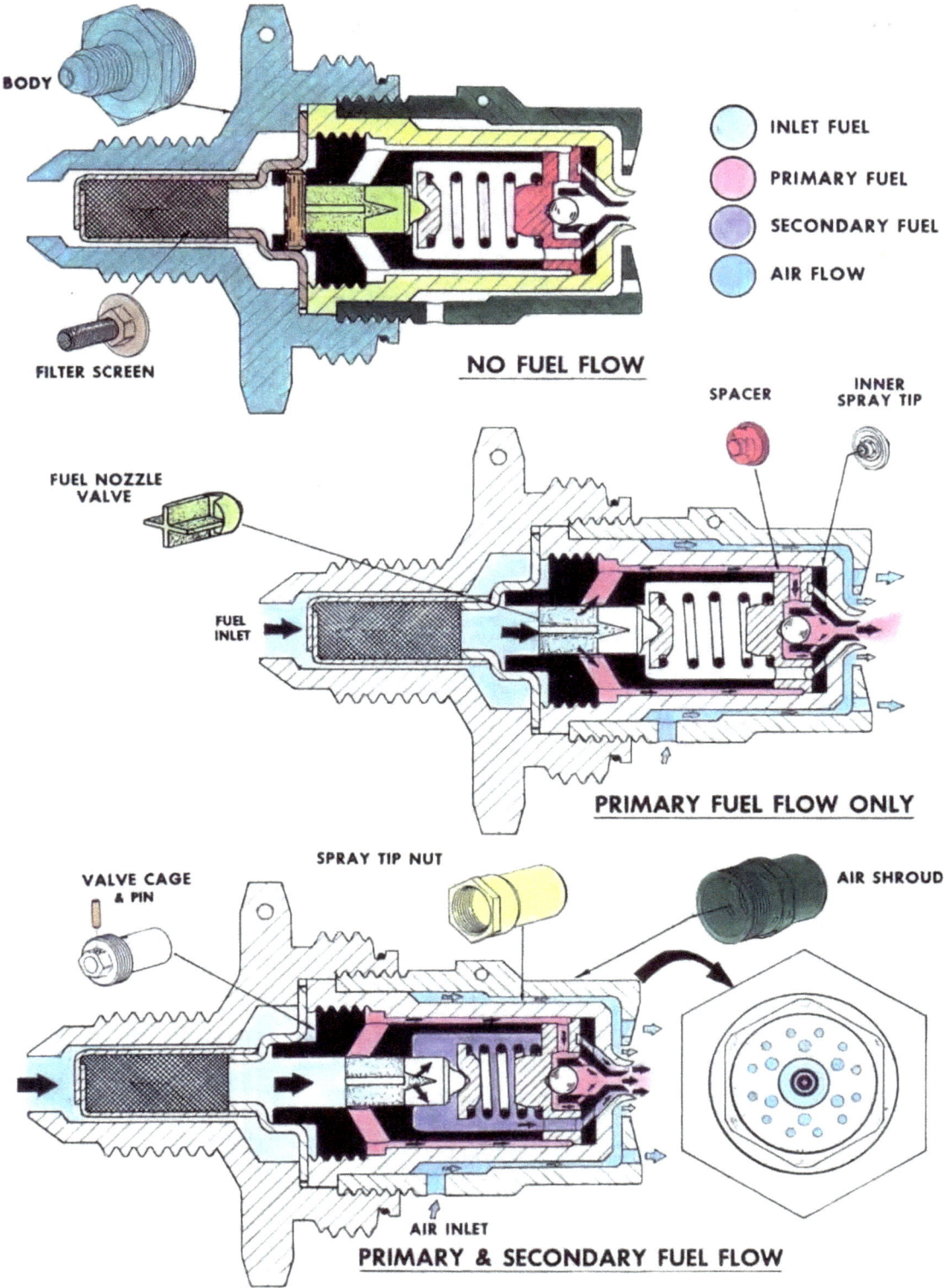

Figure 23 Duplex fuel nozzle

Plumbing

Various hoses and pipes connect the components of the fuel system. If flexible hoses are used, they are constructed of an inner rubber with an out wire shielding with another layer of insulated fire-resistant rubber-coated material. Purpose-built pipes are made of stainless steel.

It is important during the pre-flight inspection that any unusual wear, nicks, cuts, scratches, discolouring etc. are brought to the attention of an engineer.

Turbine Engine Fuel

The energy used in our aircraft engines came initially from the sun, which is our main source of energy. Heat energy was changed to chemical energy millions of years ago by the photosynthesis of plant life. Then through the ages, the plants and animals have been buried under the earth. Eventually, through heat and pressure acting on them, they have become the petroleum products that we use today. This may be a rough description, but it gives you the idea.

The following diagram shows how heat energy from the sun is eventually changed into mechanical energy.

| Energy arrives from the sun | Energy is stored as a chemical | Fuel burns to provide heat | Heat is converted into mechanical energy in an engine |

The function of fuel is to provide the energy for us to harness and convert to power.

The function of the fuel system is to store the fuel and deliver it to the FCU so it can then be used by the engine in the process of converting chemical energy into mechanical energy.

Fuel Types

There are two basic fuel types. A gasoline or petrol type of fuel with high volatility is used in piston engines, and a kerosene-type fuel with lower volatility is used in diesel and gas turbine engines.

Early turbine engines used straight kerosene or diesel as they met the basic burning requirements of the engines of the time, however as operational demands and engine sophistication increased, turbine fuels have been specifically developed to give specific burning characteristics, optimum storage qualities, much better quality control ensuring clean fuel, and better resistance to the formation of ice and the growth of microbiological (fungal) organisms.

In aviation, both types (petrol and kerosene) of fuel are used, depending on the type of engine installed in the helicopter.

Figure 24 Piston engines use AVGAS

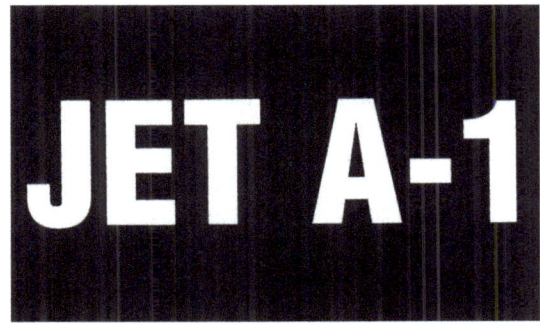

Figure 25 Turbine engines use AVTUR

It is important to note that turbine engines can be run on either fuel type dependent on the manufacturers' recommendations. In fact, once started, the turbine engine can operate adequately on diesel, AVGAS, MOGAS, natural gas, industrial or lamp kerosene, turpentine, or just about anything that can burn. However, because the quality of these fuels is not as strict as with aviation fuel, contaminants that enter the fuel system will block filters, and clog FCUs. Also, the different burning characteristics and the differing specific gravities of each of these fuels may upset the metering and delivering of the fuel via the FCU and cause temperature and power fluctuations. In general, in an emergency, differing fuels may be used for a short time in turbine engines. Make sure that the fuel is pumped in through a filter to ensure it is as clean as possible. After the flight, the engine will have to then be inspected by an engineer to determine if any long-term damage has been done.

Turbine Fuel Characteristics

Fuel for a gas turbine engine should ideally have the following characteristics:

- Flow easily under all operating conditions.
- Permit engine starting under all ground conditions and satisfactory in-flight relight.
- Have efficient combustion.
- High calorific value (energy content per pound measured in BTU).
- Have minimal harmful effects on the turbine blades.
- Have minimal corrosive effects on the fuel system components.
- Provide sufficient lubrication for the moving parts of the fuel system.
- Reduce fire hazards to a minimum.
- Not hold water in suspension.
- Have a low freezing point.

Fuels are coloured for identification

Fuel Name	Grade	Colour	Engine type
AVGAS	100/130	Green	Piston
AVGAS	100LL	Blue	Piston
MOGAS	80/87	Red	Piston
AVTUR	Kerosene	Clear	Turbine

AVTUR may be pale yellow if containing certain additives. It is important to understand that if fuels are mixed their colour may change. For example, if you mix AVGAS 100LL (Low Lead) which is blue with MOGAS which is red the fuel may become clear and look similar to water or AVTUR.

Types of Jet Fuel

Aviation Jet Fuel is commonly known as AVTUR (Aviation Turbine). The most common blend is Jet-A1. This also has the military designation F-35. In the USA Jet-A1 is also known as JP-5 (Jet Petroleum – 5).

Another blend of AVTUR commonly available (particularly in the USA) is Jet-A. In the USA Jet-A is known as JP-4 and has the military designation F-40.

These differing blends may have various additives or be refined from a different source; that is from crude oil or extracted from coal etc.

The differing additive may be for operational reasons such as working in very cold climates or in hot humid environments where fungus in the fuel tank is an issue.

Comparison chart between AVGAS and AVTUR

Below is a characteristic comparison chart between piston engine fuel and turbine engine fuel.

COMPARISON CATEGORIES	AVGAS	AVTUR
Flash point	-40	+46
Water	Will not mix	Dissolves and may freeze
Specific gravity	0.72	0.8 SG vary with temp.
Impurities	Not many	May contain some wax
Bacteria	Not many	Can pose a problem if water is present. Jet A-1 has no anti-bacterial additives. These must be added after purchase if required in Australia. The military fuel F35 does have these additives.
Calorific value	18800 BTU/pound (AVGAS is best by weight)	18600 BTU/pound (AVTUR is best by volume)
Volatility	High	Low
Altitude performance	Fuel may boil at altitude	Dissolved water may freeze
Speed of flame	760 ft/min	30 ft/min
Freezing point		-50
Spontaneous ignition temp.	725	650

Water in Turbine Fuel

Engines do not like water, so taking water out of the system is desirable. In turbine fuel, water can take one of the three following forms:

- Suspended water (sometimes referred to as entrained water) and
- Free water
- Dissolved water

There will always be some form of water in turbine fuel, it is up to the pilot to manage and minimise the amount.

Suspended Water

Tiny droplets of water can be suspended in the fuel and be floating in the system, and we are not able to see them. These small droplets will, in time, combine and form free water.

Free Water

Free water is water that we can see. It collects in the lowest part of the fuel system and is drained before the flight out of the sump into a container. Sometimes the water collects behind baffles or stagnation points and even if the pilot has completed a fuel drain, this water may remain in the system. Free water can get into the fuel tank either by being directly pumped into it during the refuelling process, by draining into it if there is a leak and it's raining, or it can simply be absorbed or drawn in through the fuel tank venting system. Often if the helicopter is left parked overnight and the fuel tank is not full, condensation can occur on the inside of the fuel tank because of the temperature changes, this water will then slide down to the bottom of the fuel tank necessitating a good fuel drain in the morning. For this reason, then it is always a good idea to fill up your fuel tank at the end of the day if it is going to be parked outside overnight.

Figure 26 Water separated from fuel

Dissolved Water

Dissolved water occurs when a molecule of water attaches itself to a molecule of hydrocarbon (fuel). This means we cannot see this water and even if the pilot has completed a fuel drain and no water is detected, water may actually still be present but held in the fuel solution. Turbine fuel can hold up to 30% water in solution with no bad side effects on the engine combustion process, however, with this amount of water in the system, temperature becomes important as the water may turn into ice at very low temperatures and ice will not flow through the fuel system.

Testing for Water

Because we cannot see suspended or dissolved water, fuel companies have produced a test kit (Figure 27) that pilots can use to test for water. This requires the pilot to take a small sample of the fuel and draw it under suction through a filter (Figure 28). If there is excess water in the system, then the filter will change colour (Figure 29 and Figure 30) and the pilot should drain the fuel out of the system and replace it with clean fuel before the flight. This can be the disadvantage of AVTUR.

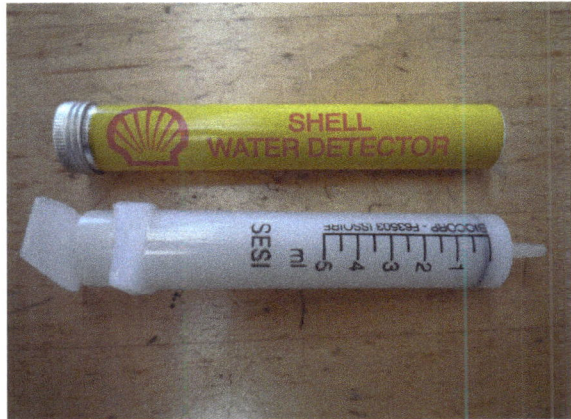

Figure 27 Syringe Testing Kit

Figure 28 Fuel being drawn under suction into a filter

Figure 29 No water detected

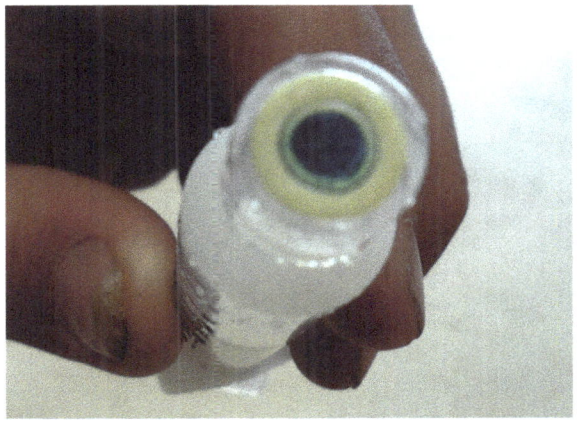

Figure 30 Water detected

Ice in Turbine Fuel

As the turbine fuel reduces to approximately -1°C to -3°C the suspended water will start to freeze and form ice crystals. This can potentially block fuel filters, fuel lines and the small holes and passages in the FCU.

Research has shown that the density of the ice crystals is approximately the same as the fuel, so the ice crystals will generally stay in suspension and float within the fuel. As the fuel temperature is further reduced it will reach the Critical Icing Temperature (CIT). At this temperature, the ice crystals will start to stick together and to their surroundings. This is when icing in the fuel starts to become a big problem.

In fixed-wing aircraft flying at very high altitudes icing is an everyday problem so the aircraft manufacturers install fuel heating devices, and the fuel supplier will put in anti-icing additives.

In helicopters, icing in fuel is not a common problem unless operating in a very cold environment in which case the manufacturer, the fuel distributor and the operator have to come up with a solution.

Heating Systems

Engines can be manufactured or installed with a fuel-oil heat exchanger. Fuel–oil heat exchangers are usually located between the fuel tank booster pumps and the fuel filter inlets. The hot oil from the engine is passed through a radiator, the fuel passes through the outside of the radiator and is warmed up, this has the added benefit of cooling the oil so it is a two-way benefit. The warm fuel resists the formation of ice.

Fuel System Icing Inhibitor (FSII)

FSII is a fuel additive that will prevent the formation of ice down to a temperature of -40°C.

It is only effective on free and suspended water as it is 500 times more soluble in water than fuel. It will migrate to undissolved water and lower its freezing point. The mixture of water and FSII has a similar density to water and will eventually either be consumed by the engine or drained out of the fuel tanks by the pilot during normal fuel drain operations.

Fuel Contamination

Turbine fuel is a very good environment for microbiological growths or more commonly referred to as fungus. This can be aggravated if free water is allowed to build up in the tank and is not drained away, which is common if an aircraft is left outside and not flown for a long time.

Fungus in the fuel tank can lead to excessive wear on fuel pumps, corrosion in the fuel system, erratic fuel quantity readings, dirty fuel, and fuel blockages.

If a fuel system has become contaminated it may have to be taken apart and cleaned. In very bad cases the entire fuel system including the fuel tank is replaced.

To prevent fungus forming, keep fuel filters clean, ensure the fuel you are putting into your helicopter is clean, always do a good fuel drain and keep water out of the system, if necessary microbiological additives can be used.

Figure 31 Fungus in a fuel tank

Turbine Engine Lubrication

Lubrication can be divided into two categories. The lubricant itself, such as the oil or grease that will reduce the friction between moving parts, and the system by which the lubricant is delivered, commonly known as the lubrication system.

Functions of Oil

Fluid lubricants (oils rather than greases) are most suitable in engines because they are easily pumped or sprayed onto or in-between surfaces, are incompressible and absorb and dissipate heat quickly. Mineral oils are used in piston engines and synthetic lubricants in turbine engines.

Reduces Friction

If you put a metal surface under a microscope you would find that its surface is not smooth but made up of many small peaks and valleys. When two surfaces then rub together, they form friction as the small bits of metal are worn away from each other. To reduce this friction; a thin film of oil is fed between moving parts, this wets the two surfaces and fills in the valleys separating the metal surfaces.

Provides Cooling

As oil moves around the engine and its components, it will absorb heat, taking the heat away from the metal parts. The heated oil is then directed through an oil cooler where the heat is transferred out to the atmosphere and the oil returned to a reservoir before repeating its purpose within the lubrication system.

Acts as a Sealant

Because oil can wet the surface it comes in contact with it acts as a sealing agent between moving parts. The thin film of oil that coats the driveshaft's and labyrinth seals increases the ability to form a tight seal. Oil will act as a sealant in many other parts of the engine.

Protection against Corrosion

When metal is left exposed, moisture and chemicals within the air can begin to form corrosion on the surfaces. Oil will not allow oxygen to reach the surface and therefore will protect against corrosion.

Cleans

Moving metal creates residue. Additionally, dirt dust, water, carbon and other contaminants may get into the engine. Oil can hold these particles within its solution and deliver them to the oil filter. The filter will then remove most of these contaminants.

Figure 32 Clean oil

Figure 33 Used oil from an engine

Types of Engine Oil

Straight Mineral Oil

Straight, natural mineral oil is used to lubricate new piston engines. It is not used for everyday use as it tends to oxidise when exposed to high temperatures or when aerated.

Metallic Ash Detergent Oil

Metallic Ash Detergent Oil (Figure 34) is a mineral oil used in piston engines with certain metallic ash-forming additives to increase the mineral oil's oxidation stability. The additives caused the carbon deposits and sludge to join together, however, they also minimised spark plug fouling, pre-ignition, and had the effect of loosening any carbon deposits and sludge so that they could be transported via the oil system to the filter. This type of oil was not very successful and is no longer used in aircraft engines due to the ash deposits it would leave in the engine.

Ashless Dispersant Oil

Ashless Dispersant Oil (Figure 35) is mineral oil with dispersant additives used in piston engines. Unlike the metallic ash detergent oil that allowed the sludge forming materials to join together, the dispersant additives cause them to repel each other and stay in suspension until they can be collected in the oil filter. Ashless Dispersant (AD) oil is approved by all aircraft engine manufacturers and is the most common form of piston engine oil in use today.

Synthetic Oil

Synthetic Oil (Figure 36) is a man-made chemical that replaces and has the same properties as mineral oil. Its biggest advantage is that it will retain its lubricating properties over a wider temperature range. It is also better at keeping the engine clean. One of its downfalls is that it seems to affect rubber seals more readily. Synthetic oil is not widely used in piston engines but is common in turbine engines.

Figure 34 Mineral oil (straight 100)   Figure 35 Ashless dispersant (W100)   Figure 36 Synthetic (Jet 254)

Compatibility

Mixing of different mineral oils should not be a problem as the basic lubricating properties are the same, the only difference being the additives. Having said this, it is not a good idea to make this a common practice. It is better for the engine to remain on the one type and the one brand of oil for its entire life. If in an emergency or if by mistake you mix mineral oils, don't be concerned. **Mixing of mineral and synthetic oils must be avoided**.

Engine Oil Properties

Viscosity

Oils are graded on their viscosity. The viscosity of a liquid is its resistance to flow and varies with temperature. Oils of lower viscosity are thin or runny and will flow easily; low viscosity oils are commonly used in cold climates. Oils of high viscosity are thick or slow and sticky and will not flow easily; high viscosity oils are commonly used in warm climates.

The clearance between the moving parts to be lubricated will determine the viscosity of the oil required to prevent the oil from breaking away and allowing the metal-to-metal contact that causes wear. The manufacturer of the engine will usually stipulate the grade of oil to use.

Oil Grades

An instrument known as a Saybolt Universal Viscosimeter measures the viscosity of oil. This instrument measures the number of seconds it takes for 60 cubic centimetres of the oil to flow through a calibrated orifice (hole) at a specified temperature. This is known as the oils SSU or Saybolt Second Universal viscosity. The Society of Automotive Engineers (SAE) and the Military (MIL) have different numbering systems for the same grade of oil but the numbers all relate to the SSU viscosity.

In-flight manuals you will read that oils that are recommended for use must meet the specifications of a MIL or SAE number. For example, the SAE rating system divides all oil into 7 groups (10 through 70) according to their viscosity. Aviation grade oil numbers are double the SAE numbers that is SAE 40 = aviation-grade 80 and SAE 50 = aviation-grade 100.

Flash Point

Flash point is the temperature to which the oil must be heated to ignite when exposed to a naked flame. The flash point of oil must be high for obvious safety reasons.

Pour Point

The pour point of oil is the lowest temperature the oil will pour without help.

Chemical Stability

Oil must resist the action of heat, moisture, acids, etc. Oil breaks down over time to form sludge, deposits, and acids.

Oils for Turbine Engines

Oils for turbine engines are a very special formulation. They are manufactured synthetically to provide a low to medium viscosity giving stability over a wide range of operating temperatures. This allows turbine engines to be started at very low temperatures (down to minus 40°C) when the oil's viscosity (thickness) is high. Once the engine is started this same oil now has to do its job under very high temperatures.

These oils are very corrosive so don't spill them on the paintwork.

Following is a list of desirable characteristics in a turbine oil

- Low volatility to minimise evaporation at high altitudes.
- Anti-foaming quality to provide more positive lubrication.
- Low lacquer and coke deposits to keep solid particle formation to a minimum.
- High flash point for safety to avoid flammable vapours that may ignite.
- Low pour point. This is the lowest temperature that an oil will gravity flow at.
- Film strength allows cohesion and adhesion.
- Wide temperature range and a high viscosity index.

Turbine Engine Lubrication System

Turbine engines have a self-contained re-circulatory lubrication system where the oil is stored in a reservoir then distributed via pressure pumps to engine bearings, driveshafts and gear boxes and returned via a scavenge pump back to the reservoir.

The lubrication system is usually made up of a combination of the following:

- Oil tank or reservoir
- Plumbing
- Oil filter
- Oil cooler
- De-aerator
- Oil pump
- Pressure relief valves
- Chip detectors
- Scavenge pump

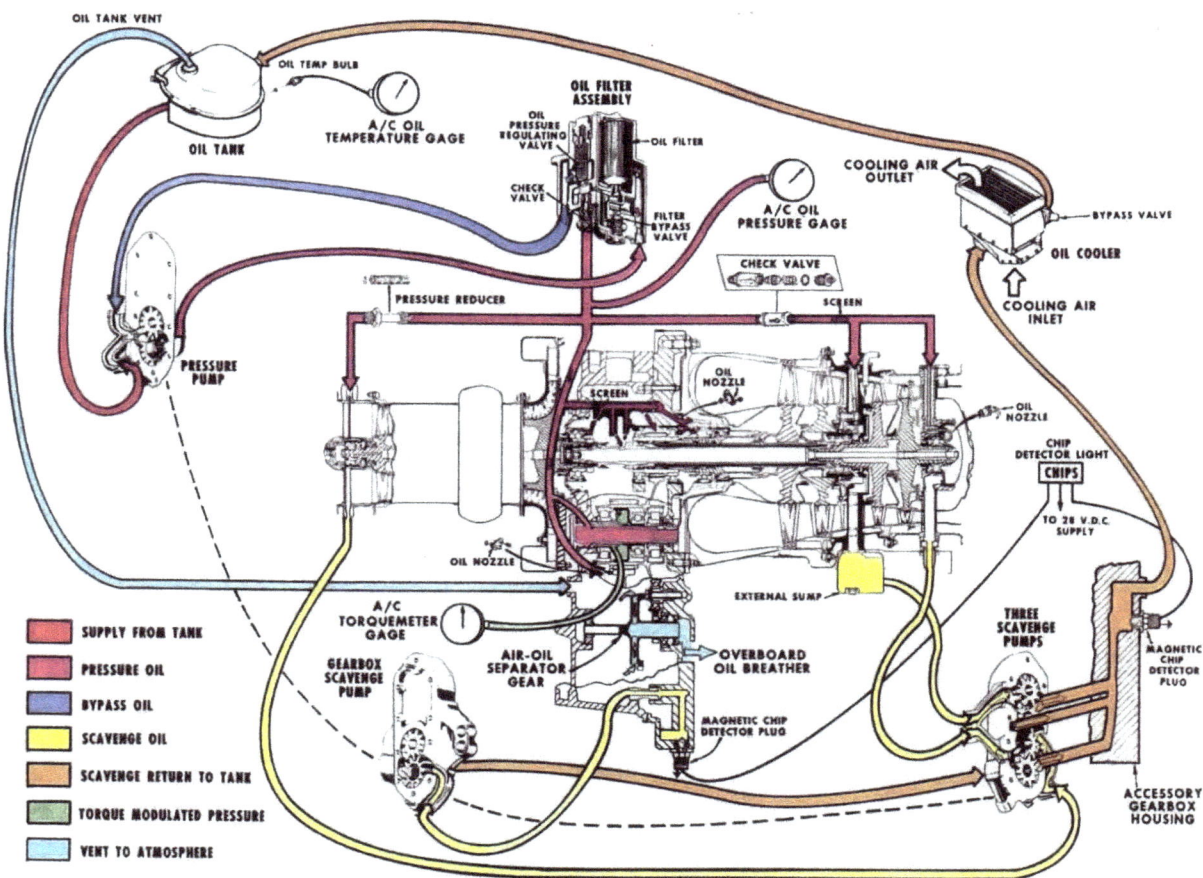

Figure 37 B206 lubrication system

There are two basic re-circulatory systems used in turbine engines, they are:

- Pressure Relief Valve system (PRV) and the
- Full Flow system.

The primary difference between the two systems is the control of the oil flow to the bearings. Pressure and temperature of the oil are critical to both systems, therefore both oil temperature and pressure will be indicated to the pilot in the cockpit.

Basic Gas Turbines for Helicopter Pilots

Pressure Relief Valve System (PRV)

A spring-loaded valve controls the oil flow to the bearing chambers in a Pressure Relief Valve (PRV) system. This valve is designed to open at a pressure that corresponds to the idling speed of the engine, therefore giving a constant feed of oil pressure over the normal engine operating RPM. At higher engine RPMs the bearing chamber pressure will increase, this reduces the pressure difference between the bearing chamber and the oil jet thereby decreasing the oil flow rate to the bearings as RPM is increased. Designers have incorporated varying valve settings with RPM however the PRV system is only suitable for turbine engines that have low bearing chamber pressure.

Full Flow System

The Full-Flow system does away with the pressure relief valve and allows an oil pressure pump to supply oil to the jets directly. As engine RPM increases so too does the pressure pump so it can keep up with RPM changes.

Components

Oil tank and de-aerator

The oil tank or reservoir can either be a standalone external unit or integrated into the engine itself. The oil tank will have refill and drain points, and a de-aerator.

The refill point usually incorporates a dipstick for determining the quantity (Figure 38). In turbine engines, the dipstick is usually calibrated to show the amount of oil that needs to be *added* rather than the amount of oil remaining. Oil consumption in a turbine is very low as the oil, unlike in a piston engine, is not involved in the combustion process. For this reason, the oil remains relatively clean and is not consumed. The drain point is for draining the oil at service time.

Figure 38 Oil tank dip stick

Because air is mixed with the oil in the bearing chambers, a de-aerating device is incorporated within the oil tank which removes the air from the oil return. To prevent excessive air pressure building up in the engine and the oil tank a vent is incorporated in the lubrication system.

Oil filter

The oil filter takes out dirt and unwanted contaminants from the oil. It can be either a paper or fine wire gauze filter. It is very similar to the fuel filter in that if it becomes blocked there will be a bypass valve and an indication to the pilot. This may take the form of a warning light on the instrument console or a pop-up indicator on the filter itself that the pilot or engineer should check during the helicopter's daily pre-flight inspection.

If the oil filter does become blocked and the oil bypasses the filter, then oil temperatures may increase and oil pressure may be at a constant higher value.

Oil cooler

A radiator type filter has air forced through it taking away the heat from the oil. In fixed-wing, the ram air from forward movement provides most of the cooling air, in helicopters however the oil needs to be cooled while at the hover so either an electric fan or a belt-driven fan is used to force the air through the radiator.

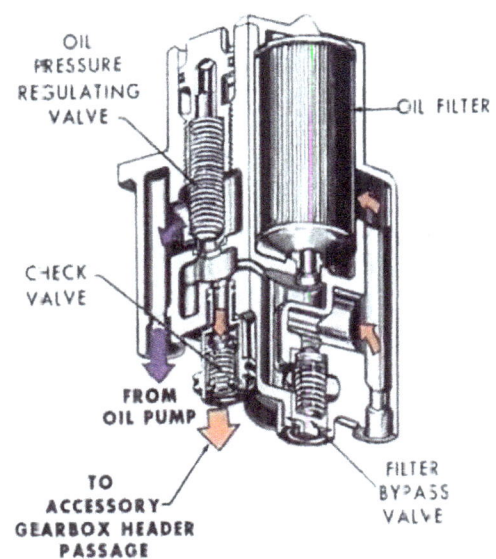

Figure 39 Oil filter schematic

Plumbing

Various hoses and pipes connect all the components of the oil system. Like the plumbing in the fuel system, they must all be inspected during the daily pre-flight.

Oil pump

The oil pump is a vital component of the lubrication system. A failure of the oil pump will lead to a failure of the engine, therefore the driveshafts that power the oil pumps do not have a weak shear point, allowing the pump to continue to provide oil pressure for as long as possible even after it is damaged.

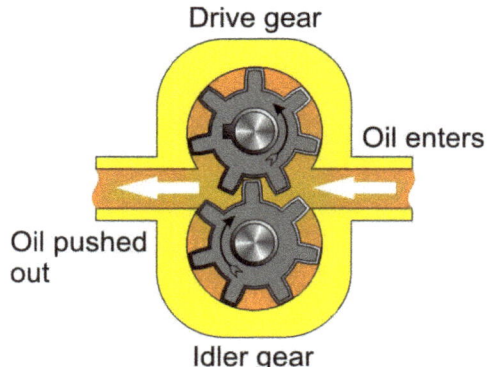

The gear pump is driven by a driveshaft in the accessories gearbox of the engine. The driveshaft turns the drive gear that spins around. The drive gear through its rotation turns the idler gear so that the two work in unison.

As oil enters the pump the gears are opening and making larger the entry space as they rotate. This makes more room for oil to come in. The oil enters and is then picked up by the gears and carried around the outside of the gears to the outlet where the gears are closing together and making smaller the exit space, therefore pushing the oil out with force giving pressure.

Figure 40 Oil gear pump schematic

Pressure relief valves for protection

If an oil cooler or filter becomes blocked, to prevent the pressure pump from continually providing oil into the unit until it literally bursts, pressure relief valves are fitted so that the oil can bypass these systems. This allows the oil to still lubricate the bearings and driveshaft's, but it will just not be filtered or cooled.

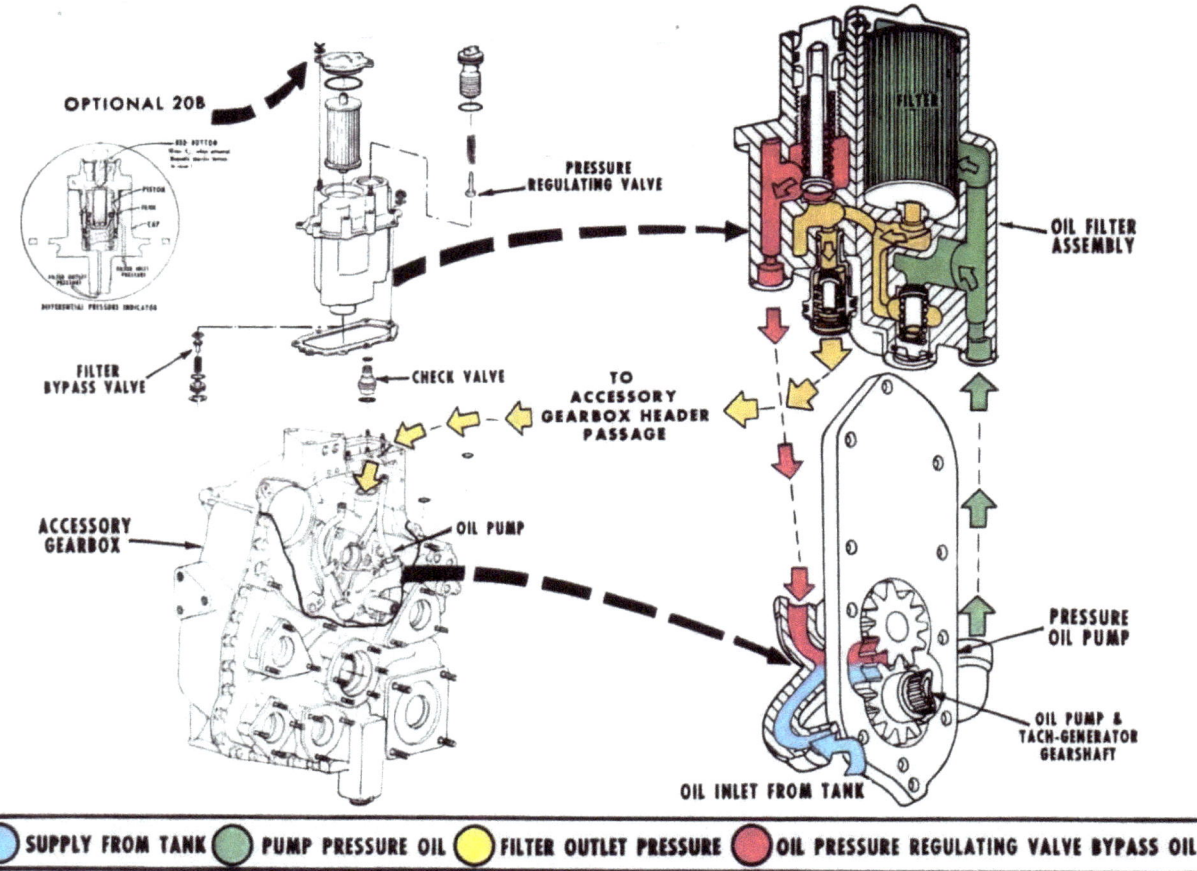

A differential pressure switch located at the filter will sense an increase in the pressure difference between the inlet and outlet sides of the filter. This is usually transmitted to the warning panel to notify the pilot of the blockage. In the event of a blockage of the filter or the cooler, oil temperatures may rise, oil pressure in the system may increase and the pilot should return to base for servicing.

Chip detectors

A chip plug is a small magnet placed in the oil line, (usually close to the pump as that is where metal may come from) that will pick up any ferrous metal that is usually an indication of a bearing or pump failure. If the magnet does pick up metal it will cause a circuit to close and a warning light to activate in the cockpit. Some chip plugs are not connected to a warning light system and can be inspected by the pilot before a flight. If metal is found it should be kept and shown to an engineer. Chip plugs should be handled with care and cleaned with a clean rag.

In helicopters, chip plugs may be installed in the engine oil system, hydraulic system, main and tail rotor gear boxes. Each chip plug will work independently and be designed for that particular system.

Below is an example of a chip plug system in a Squirrel AS350 hydraulic system.

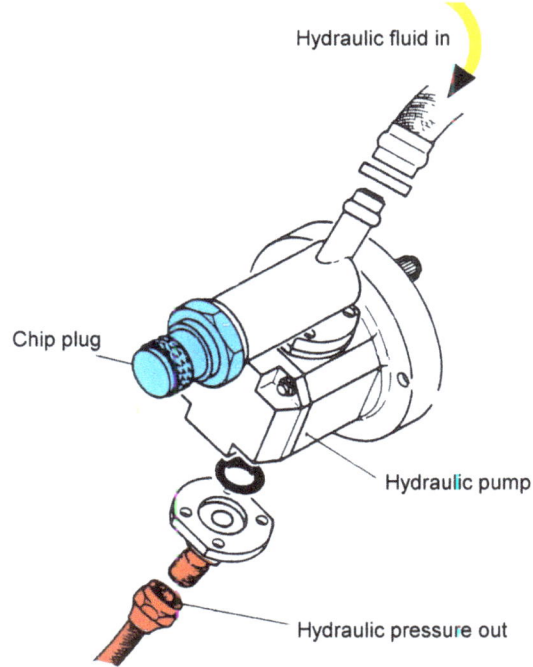

Figure 41 AS350 Squirrel hydraulic system chip plug schematic

Figure 42 Chip plug in

Figure 43 Chip plug cut

Turbine Engine Sealing

Because turbine engines run at such high RPMs and because they rely on a constant reliable flow of air, fuel and oil to operate properly, then well-designed seals are a necessity.

Seals in turbine engines are used for three main purposes:

- To control the cooling airflow.
- To provide an additional barrier in preventing the combustion gases from passing through the turbine disc cavities.
- To prevent oil leaking from the engine bearing chambers.

It is important to remember that oil itself is a sealant and will assist the physical seals to do their job.

Types of seals

The types of seals used in turbine engines include:

- Labyrinth seals
- Carbon seals
- Ring seals
- Hydraulic
- Brush seals

The type of seal used will be dependent on the surrounding temperatures and pressures it will have to work in. Additionally, resistance to wear, the amount of heat the seal itself may generate, the amount of space available for installation, ease of manufacture, periodic installation and removal are all key elements in deciding the best type of seal to use in a particular situation.

Labyrinth Seals

The labyrinth seal is the most common form of seal used in a turbine engine. Comprising of a series of fins or blades, which rub against the relatively softer abradable lining of the opposing surface; this will cause a fine cut or groove giving a minimum clearance between the fixed and the rotating parts.

[11]

[12]

Across each sealing fin or blade, there is a small pressure drop that restricts the flow of sealing air or oil from one side of the seal to the other. When a labyrinth seal is used for oil-bearing chambers, oil leakage is prevented by airflow from the outside to the inside of the chamber. This flow also induces a positive pressure which assists the oil return system.

Carbon Seals

A carbon seal (Figure 44) consists of a static ring of carbon segments that are held in place by springs. The carbon seal will continuously rub against a collar on a rotating shaft which will prevent oil or air loss.

The heat generated by the friction of the carbon seal rubbing against the collar is taken away by the engine oil system.

Ring Seals

A ring seal (Figure 45) consists of a metal ring housed in a close-fitting static groove. The clearance between the ring and the rotating shaft is normally smaller than that which can be obtained by using a labyrinth seal because the ring is free to rotate in its housing whenever the spinning shaft comes into contact with it. Ring seals are used for bearing chamber sealing except in very hot areas where oil degradation could lead to the ring becoming seized within its housing.

Hydraulic Seals

Hydraulic seals (Figure 46) are formed by the tip of a sealing fin penetrating the surface of an annulus of oil which has been created by centrifugal force.

Hydraulic seals are often used between two rotating components to seal a bearing chamber. Unlike labyrinth and ring seals, the hydraulic seal does not allow a controlled flow of air across the seal. Any differences in air pressure inside and outside of the bearing chamber are compensated for by a difference in oil level on each side of the fin.

Brush Seals

Brush seals (Figure 47) comprise a static ring of fine wire bristles which are continuously rubbing against a collar of hard ceramic material on a rotating shaft.

The brush seal copes well with any rubbing caused by a shaft flexing without increasing leakage.

Figure 44 Carbon seals[13]

Figure 45 Ring seals[14]

Figure 46 Hydraulic seals

Figure 47 Brush seals[15]

Turbine Engine Starting, Ignition and Shutdown

The gas turbine engine is started by rotating the turbine/compressor via a starter motor, which is being powered by a battery or another power source.

The starter motor must accelerate the compressor to provide sufficient air, under pressure, to support combustion in the combustion chamber, as well as give enough cooling air so that the turbine is not damaged during the start cycle.

Once fuel has been introduced, the igniter system must be powerful enough to produce a spark that will ignite the fuel-air mixture already under pressure and at a high velocity. Once ignition has occurred, the compressor is still providing high amounts of drag such that the turbine is not able to continue to accelerate, therefore the starter motor must continue to assist the engine to a self-sustaining speed.

The torque supplied by the starter motor must be well in excess of that required to overcome friction and air loads during the start sequence.

To start a turbine engine two systems are required:

- A starter system to initially rotate the high-pressure compressor/turbine spool and
- An ignition system.

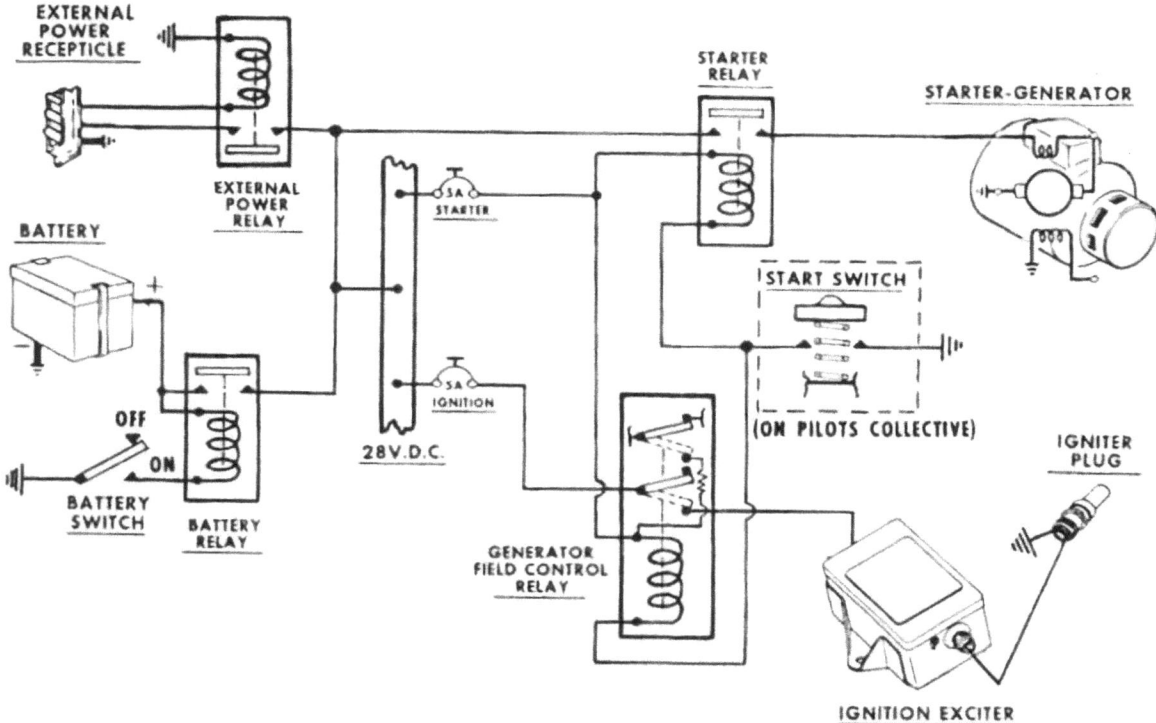

Starter System

In general, the starting system can either be fully automatic, partially automatic or manual (also known as modulated).

In a fully automatic system (FADEC), the pilot does very little but monitors the starting parameters. If the start cycle is disrupted or not normal, the start switch is selected to off and the fuel shut off valve is selected to off, thereby aborting the start. All other parameters will be controlled by the aircraft's onboard computer.

In a partially automatic system, the pilot normally manages the N1 compressor speed and the timing of the introduction of the fuel and therefore ignition. Once the fuel is introduced and ignited the FCU then determines the correct amount of fuel for the start. In the event of an abnormal start, the pilot will take away the fuel thereby aborting the start. This is called a Bendix system in the B206BIII.

In a manual or modulated start the pilot manages the N1 compressor speed, the timing of the introduction of the fuel and therefore ignition and then the quantities of fuel into the combustion chamber to directly control the turbine temperature and therefore modulate the start. In the event of an abnormal start, the pilot will take away the fuel thereby aborting the start. This is known as the CECO (Chandler Evans Company) in the B206BIII.

In helicopters, any of the above starting methods could be utilised depending on the helicopter's design and sophistication.

Basic Starting Components

Starter motor

Connected to a battery, the starter motor is a small electric motor usually connected to the accessories gearbox. When the pilot activates the starter motor, either by depressing and holding down a button in the cockpit or by telling a computer to commence the start sequence (FADEC) the starter motor will start working. This rotary motion is transmitted by gears through the accessories gearbox to the N1 Gas Producer Turbine wheel which in turn is connected to the compressor. The compressor will then start drawing air into the engine and the combustion chamber.

When the compressor reaches a predetermined percentage (this is determined by the manufacturer) the pilot can then introduce fuel and allow ignition. For example, 12-15% in the B206BIII.

The starter motor has to provide sufficient torque to drive the cold accessories gearbox and overcome the large amount of drag produced by the compressor. Once started the turbine engine will require assistance from the starter motor to help it to accelerate to its self-sustaining speed which is approximately 35-50% of its ground idle RPM.

It helps then if the starter motor is powered by a good battery.

Battery

The battery is very important in a turbine for starting. The problem is powerful batteries are usually very heavy and the last thing we want in a helicopter is to be carrying around a big heavy battery for only one or two starts.

For this reason, helicopter batteries are usually small but of sufficient power to attempt one and possibly two attempts at a start. Any more than that and the battery has usually been drained and a third attempt is often not possible.

Ground power units are therefore very useful in providing the high amperage required to start a turbine engine. In most cases, a minimum of 300 CCA (Cold Cranking Amps) are required to start a small turbine engine.

Lead-acid, sealed gel or NiCad batteries are all utilised in helicopters.

Ignition System

The ignition of the fuel-air mix in the combustion chamber is provided by the electric spark of an igniter plug which receives its current from an ignition exciter commonly referred to as the igniter box. This box may be either DC or AC dependent on design.

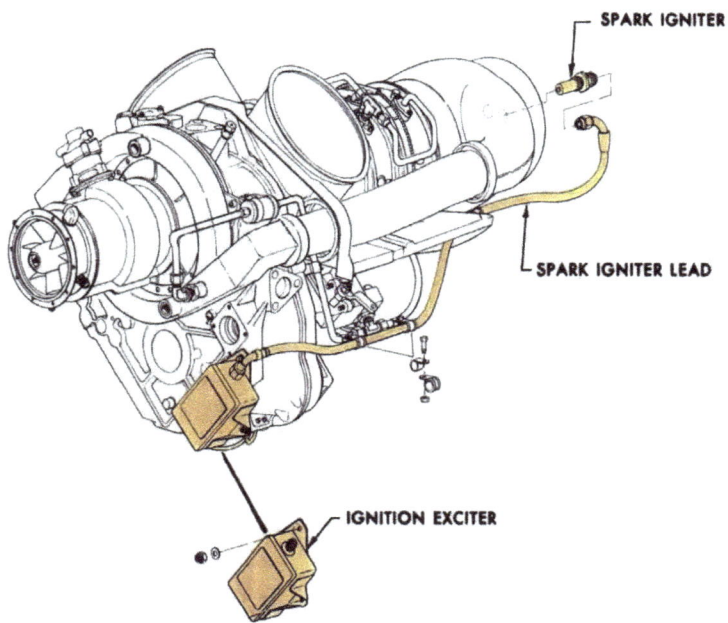

Ignition Components

Igniter plug

The igniter plug will provide a high voltage spark in the vicinity of 20,000 volts to ignite the fuel-air mix. Once the starter button is depressed you can hear a regular "ticking" at the rate of 1 – 2 beats per second. This is the igniter plug and as a pilot, you should listen for it. If the plug is not going then the engine will not start.

Under no circumstances should this type of igniter be cleaned by wire brushing, sand blasting, and vapour blasting or scraping of the tip. Any of these operations can damage the conducting material which is present between the electrodes and result in the igniter becoming inoperative or reducing its useful life.

If you remove a plug and find a lump of carbon on its tip, the lump can be removed with a blunt instrument with care taken not to damage the conducting material. Normal soot or carbon formation on the tip of the igniter is not detrimental to its operation and it need not be removed. If cleaning is required or desired, then it is recommended that it is only wiped with a soft cloth.

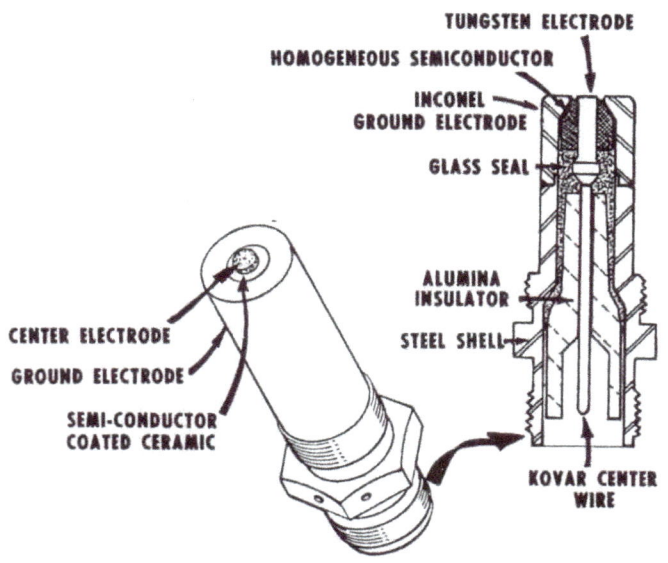

To prolong the life of the igniter, once the engine has completed its start cycle, the igniter will stop functioning and lie dormant until either the auto re-light system activates, the pilot manually depresses the start button in flight, or the pilot attempts another engine start.

Igniter box

The high energy ignition box receives a low voltage supply controlled by the starting electrical circuit from the helicopter's electrical system. The electrical energy is stored in the unit until it is delivered as a high voltage, high amperage discharge across the igniter plug.

After a start cycle has been completed the capacitors inside the igniter box can retain a residual electrical charge for up to 5 minutes before it is dissipated. This may be in the vicinity of 20,000 volts, therefore, after a start, do not touch the igniter box.

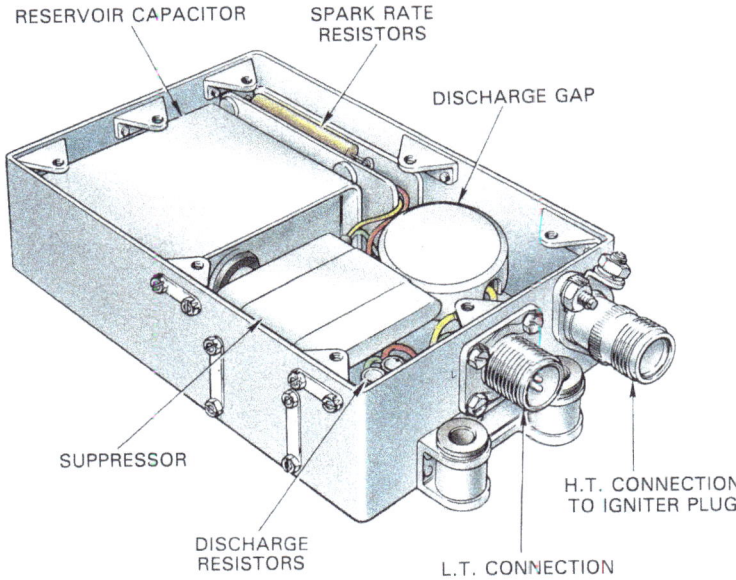

Igniter leads or harness

Connecting the two other components, this cable must be well shielded, and care should be taken to check it during the pre-flight. Wear or breaks in the shielding may lead to arcing which could start a fire, failure of the igniter plug to ignite the fuel-air mixture and radio interference.

Starting Problems

Hot Starts

A hot start is a condition when a turbine engine starts but its internal gas temperature rapidly rises to the point of exceeding the start limitations causing damage to the engine.

This is a potentially dangerous and damaging situation and may be caused by any one or more of the following:

- Low battery voltage, leading to insufficient torque output from the starter motor. This could be either the aircraft's battery or the ground power unit.
- Premature cut out of the starter motor. This may be due to pilot error by releasing the start button before reaching the turbine self-sustaining speed or due to a malfunction in the FADEC or FCU.
- Insufficient torque from the starter motor due to excessive wear on the starter generator brushes.
- Light up occurring too early with compressor speeds too low. This may be due to pilot error or FADEC issues.
- Compressor or turbine defects.
- A strong tail wind which blows the hot exhaust gases back into the turbine as well as recirculating the hot exhaust gas back through the intake.
- A start with the engine already hot. This may be due to a recent shutdown and the static engine temperature still up around 200-300°C before start. In most turbines, a limit of 150°C is given before ignition is permitted.
- Too much fuel. This may be due to pilot error (such as conducting a wet start) or FADEC or FCU issues.

If a hot start is being experienced it is imperative that the fuel supply is cut off immediately. Additionally, the pilot is to ensure that the starter motor continues to crank the engine, venting the hot gases out through the exhaust. Once the temperature has reduced, the flame extinguished and there is no further possibility of an over-temperature the starter button may then be released. This extra cranking will also expel any unburnt fuel.

Because a hot start can happen very quickly it is crucial that the pilot monitors the engine instruments and focuses on the engine start until the self-sustaining RPM is reached.

Engine indications in the cockpit will to some degree lag behind actual turbine gas temperatures. This is most evident during a hot start. For this reason, reading the trend of the turbine temperature is just as important as the actual value is displayed.

Pilots should know by memory the temperature limitations for the specific turbine about to be started.

Hung Starts

A hung start is a condition where the engine starts but then fails to accelerate up to ground idle RPM.

This may be caused by one or more of the following:

- The battery voltage weakening, leading to the starter motor not providing the torque required to assist the engine up to ground idle.
- Premature cut out of the starter motor either due to pilot error or a failure of the starter motor.
- A problem in the FADEC or FCU where fuel is not continually increased to accelerate the engine.
- A problem with the compressor inlet guide vanes or bleed valve system, leading to excessive back pressure through the compressor stages.

If a hung start is being experienced then cut off the fuel supply but continue to motor the engine until the turbine temperatures have reduced.

Wet Start

This is when no light up occurs after fuel is introduced during the start sequence. Faulty igniters are usually the cause or the igniter has been deactivated and the pilot did not notice. Subsequently, fuel is left in the can and must be drained before attempting another start. This may be done by waiting for 5 or more minutes and the fuel will drain out of a drain pipe, or the pilot could conduct dry motoring run with the igniters deactivated.

If the pilot aborts the start because of no ignition, then immediately discovers the problem and attempts another start immediately without a dry run, or waiting for the fuel to drain, then the igniter will ignite the stagnant fuel in the combustion chamber before the RPM has increased to start RPM. This will result in a hot start.

Engine Relight

If the flame in the combustion chamber goes out in flight, then the turbine will very quickly spool down. This is known as a flame out and is in effect an engine failure necessitating an autorotation.

It would be a good design feature to be able to relight the engine in flight. This is either done through an automatic re-light or re-ignition system. If the aircraft does not have an automatic re-light system then it is done manually by the pilot.

The flame may go out in the combustion chamber for one or more of the following reasons:

- Water in the fuel.
- Dirty fuel.
- Excessive water coming in through the intake system (heavy rain, or snow).
- Problems with the airflow caused by intake ice, damaged compressor, faulty bleed valve or leakage in the plumbing (transfer tubes).
- Problems with the fuel either due to fuel starvation because of mismanagement by the pilot (tank selection), fuel pump problems or vapour locks, faulty FCU or FADEC or air leaks in the fuel.
- Problems with the fuel nozzle.
- Altitude is too high (no air!).

If the flame does go out, RPM will quickly decay. Once the N1 RPM gets below a pre determined value an auto re-light system will automatically cause the igniter to start activating, this should automatically relight the flame and restore engine RPM as fuel is still being pumped into the combustion chamber.

In a manual system, the pilot is required to retard the throttle to off, wait till the N1 gets down to the low start value then conduct a normal start. In a fixed-wing, this is an option, as high flying fixed-wing have time to go through drills, checks and start cycles. In helicopters, flying close to the ground is usually not an option; therefore, if an auto re-light system is not installed it is not recommended to waste valuable time that should be spent conducting an autorotation in attempting a manual re-light.

Engine Shutdown

To shut down a turbine engine all that is required is to take away the fuel. This can be done by retarding (rolling off) the throttle to the off position.

Different manufacturers have varying requirements with regards to cooling down to minimise the possibility of thermal shock.

American designed turbine engines typically require a 2 minute cool down time.

European designed turbine engines typically require 0 – 30 seconds of cool down time.

Once the fuel is shut off the RPM and turbine temperature will drop immediately. This is not a time to relax, however, as a turbine engine can experience a hot shutdown.

Hot Shutdown

If fuel is allowed back into the combustion chamber after shutdown then the flame may re-ignite and turbine temperatures rapidly increase just like they may in a hot start.

Pilot vigilance and attention to the gauges are just as essential during a shutdown as it is for a start.

Fuel may be unintentionally reintroduced into the combustion chamber by one or more of the following:

- The pilot mismanaging the throttle and rolling it on again. This may only be by a small amount. If dual controls are installed it is not uncommon for the exiting pilot or passenger to accidentally roll on some throttle and thereby allow fuel back into the combustion chamber.
- Faulty FADEC or FCU.

If a hot shut down is being experienced, immediately depress the starter button to motor over the engine, check that the throttle is fully off, deactivate the igniter (switch off or pull the circuit breaker) and select the main fuel valve to OFF.

Continue to dry motor the engine until the temperatures have stabilised.

BGT Terminology

Below are a list of common terms and their definitions as they relate to turbine engines.

Term	Definition
Aborted Start	Termination of the engine starting cycle when combustion (light-off) does not occur within a prescribed time limit.
Acceleration Due to Gravity	The acceleration of a freely falling body due to the attraction of gravity expressed as the rate of increase of velocity per unit of time. In a vacuum, the rate is 32.2 feet per second squared (9.8 meters per second squared) near sea level.
Absolute Pressure	A pressure measured in reference to a complete vacuum. It is distinguished from gauge pressure by suffixing an "a" to the indicated pressure, i.e. psia or Hga.
Absolute Temperature	Measured from zero degrees absolute on all scales. It is a theoretical point where there is presumed to be no molecular activity and hence no heat. (-273.1°C or -459.6°F)
Accessory Drive Gearbox	Also called Main Gearbox. Provides mounting space and drive for engine accessories.
Adiabatic	An adiabatic temperature change occurs without the addition or removal of heat, such as the drop in temperature that occurs when a gas under pressure is released to lower pressure.
Afterburner	A tubular combustion chamber with a variable size exhaust outlet attached to the rear of a gas turbine engine into which fuel is injected through a set of spray bars. The burning of fuel in the exhaust supplements the normal thrust of the engine by increasing the acceleration of the air mass through an additional temperature rise.
Aerofoil	Any surface designed to obtain a useful reaction upon its surfaces from the air through which it moves. Velocity increases over the cambered side producing lift on the underside.
Ambient	Refers to the condition of the atmosphere existing around the engine, such as ambient pressure or temperature.
Ambient Air	The atmospheric air surrounding all sides of the aircraft or engine. Expressed in terms of lbs/sq. inch or in. Hg.
Annular Combustor	A cylindrical one-piece combustion chamber sometimes referred to as a single basket type combustor.
Auxiliary Power Unit (APU)	A type of gas turbine, usually located in the aircraft fuselage, whose purpose is to provide either electrical power, air pressure for starting main engines, or both. Similar in design to ground power units.
Axial	Motion along a real or imaginary straight line on which an object supposedly or actually rotates. The engine centre line.
Axial Flow Compressor	Compressor with airflow parallel to the axis of the engine. The numerous compressor stages raise the pressure of the air but essentially make no change in direction of airflow.

Term	Definition
Barometric Pressure	Atmospheric (absolute) pressure. At sea level, the standard barometric pressure is 29.92 "HgA. (14.7 psia). Barometric pressure is the result of gravitational attraction (weight) of the atmospheric gases and decreases with altitude.
Bernoulli Effect	The reduced pressure existing in the throat of a venturi due to the increased velocity of air in that section.
Bernoulli's Theorem	Principle which states static pressure and velocity (RAM) pressure of a gas or fluid passing through a duct (at constant subsonic flow rate) are inversely proportional, i.e. total pressure does not change.
Brayton Cycle	A thermodynamic cycle of operation that may be used to explain the operating principles of the gas turbine engine. It is sometimes referred to as the continuous combustion or constant pressure cycle.
British Thermal Unit (BTU)	The amount of heat required to raise 1 pound of pure water 1°F. One BTU = 252 Calories.
Calorie	The amount of heat required to raise 1 gram of pure water 1°C 252 Calories = One BTU.
Can-Annular Combustor	A set, generally of 6 to 10 liners within one outer annulus (combustor outer case).
Centigrade Temperature Scale	A temperature measuring scale in which 0°C equals the freezing point of water and 100°C equals the boiling point of water, at sea level, on a standard day (29.92 "Hg).
Centrifugal Flow Compressor	An impeller shaped device that receives air at its centre and slings air outwards at high velocity into a diffuser to increase pressure. Sometimes referred to as a radial outflow compressor.
Choked Airflow	An airflow condition from a convergent shaped nozzle, where the gas is travelling at the speed of sound and cannot be further accelerated. Any increase in internal pressure will pass out the nozzle in the form of pressure.
Combustor	The section of the engine into which fuel is injected and burned to create the expansion of the gases.
Compressor	An impeller or a multi-bladed rotor assembly. A component that is driven by a turbine rotor to compress incoming air.
Compressor Pressure Ratio	The result of compressor discharge pressure divided by compressor inlet pressure, eg. A large turbofan may have a compressor pressure ratio of 25:1.
Compressor Stage	A rotor blade set followed by a stator vane set. Simply stated, the rotating aerofoils create air velocity which then changes to pressure in the numerous diverging ducts formed by the stator vanes.
Compressor Stall	A condition in an axial flow compressor in which one or more stages of rotor blades fail to pass air smoothly to the succeeding stages. A stall condition is caused by a pressure ratio that is incompatible with the engine RPM. Compressor stall will be indicated by a rise in EGT or RPM fluctuation, and if allowed to continue, may result in flameout and physical damage to the engine.

Term	Definition
Convergent Duct	A cone-shaped passage or channel in which a gas may be made to flow from its largest area to its smallest area, resulting in an increase in velocity and a decrease in pressure. Referred to as nozzle shaped. With the relationship present, the weight of airflow will remain constant.
Diffuser	The divergent section of the engine used to convert the velocity energy in the compressor discharge air to pressure energy. Aircraft inlet ducts and compressor stator vanes are also described as diffusers due to their effect on the air in raising pressure.
Directional Reference	An industry standard to describe engine locations. The orientation is to look from the rear towards the front of the engine and use standard twelve-hour clock reference points. The right side and left side are also determined in this manner.
Divergent Duct	A cone-shaped passage or channel in which a gas may be made to flow from its smallest to its largest area resulting in an increase in pressure and a decrease in velocity. With this relationship present, the weight or airflow remains constant, e.g. the engine diffuser.
Dual Spool Compressor	A design utilising two independently rotating compressors. The front compressor is referred to as the Low Pressure (LP) Compressor while the rear is referred to as the High Pressure (HP) Compressor.
Energy	Inherent power or the capacity for performing work. When a portion of matter is stationary, it often has energy due to its position in relation to other portions of matter. This is called potential energy. If the matter is moving, it is said to have kinetic energy or energy due to motion.
Engine Cycle	Cycles are recorded as one take-off and landing and are used to compute time between overhaul of engines and components where operating hours are not used.
Engine Pressure Ratio (EPR)	The ratio of turbine discharge pressure divided by compressor inlet pressure. Displayed in the cockpit as an indication of engine thrust.
Engine Stations	Numbered locations along the engine length, or along the gas path used to identify pressure and temperature points, component locations and the like.
Exhaust Gas Temperature (EGT)	Temperature taken at the turbine exit. Often referred to as T_{t7}.
Exhaust Nozzle	Also referred to as the jet nozzle, this is the rear most of the engine.
Flame Out	An unintentional extinction of combustion due to a blowout (too much fuel) or die out (too little fuel).
Foreign Object Damage (FOD)	Compressor damage from ingestion of foreign objects into the engine inlet.
Free Power Turbine	A turbine wheel that drives a power output gearbox rather than a compressor. Found in turboprop and turboshaft engines.
Fuel Control Unit (FCU)	The main fuel scheduling device that receives a mechanical input signal from the power lever and various other signals such as P_{t2}, T_{t2}, etc. These signals provide for automatic scheduling of fuel at all ambient conditions of ground and flight operation.
Fuel Flow	The rate at which fuel is consumed by the engine in pounds per hour (pph).
Gas Generator Turbine	High-pressure turbine wheel/s which drive the compressor of a turboprop or turboshaft engine.

Term	Definition
Gauge Pressure	A pressure measured in reference to the surrounding ambient pressure, ambient pressure being 0 psia. It is distinguished from absolute pressure by suffixing a "g" to the indicated pressure (psig) where necessary.
Gross Thrust	The thrust developed by the engine, ignoring any initial air mass movement, regardless of flight conditions.
Ground Power Unit	A type of small gas turbine whose purpose is to provide either electrical power, air pressure for starting aircraft engines, or both. A ground power unit is connected to the aircraft when needed. Similar to an aircraft installed APU.
High-Pressure Turbine	The turbine rotor that drives the high-pressure compressor in a dual or triple spool axial flow gas turbine engine.
Heat	The energy possessed by matter resulting from the motion of the matter's molecules. The faster the motion of the molecules, the greater the energy present and the higher the temperature. Two factors must be considered, the intensity measured as temperature, and quantity, as measured in BTUs.
Heat of Compression	The amount of heat added to a gas by the act of compression alone; hence an adiabatic change. It can be measured by subtracting the enthalpy of 1 pound of gas at the compressor intake from the enthalpy of the same pound of gas at the compressor discharge.
Horsepower	Unit of power equal to 33,000 foot-pounds of work per minute, 550 foot-pounds per second, or 375 mile-pounds per hour.
Hot Start	Over-temperature during engine start. A start that occurs with normal engine rotation, but EGT exceeds prescribed limits. This is usually caused by an excessively rich mixture in the combustor. The fuel to the engine must be terminated immediately to prevent engine damage.
Hung Start	Failure to reach normal idling RPM during engine starting. A condition of normal light-off but with RPM remaining at some low value rather than increasing to the normal idle RPM. This is often the result of insufficient power to the engine from the starter. In the event of a hung start, the engine should be shut down.
Idle	A percent RPM setting, the value of which changes from engine to engine. It is the lowest engine operating speed authorised.
Inertia	The property of matter to resist any change in its state of rest or uniform motion.
Latent Heat	The heat required to change the state of matter, such as from a liquid to gas. Measured in BTUs per pound, it cannot be sensed or measured as a temperature change.
Latent Heat of Vaporisation	The amount of heat required to change the state of a liquid, at the boiling point, to a gas at the same temperature. The heat of vaporisation for water is 970 BTUs per pound. Heat condensation is the term applied when the change of state is from a gas to a liquid and heat is released.
Low-Pressure Turbine	The turbine rotor that drives the low-pressure compressor in a dual or triple spool axial flow gas turbine engine.
Match Number	The ratio of the speed of the aircraft to the speed of sound (at the temperature at which the aircraft is operating).
Mass	The amount of matter contained within a substance.

Term	Definition
Mass Flow	The weight of a substance, such as air flowing past a given point in a given period of time, e.g. 10 lbs of air per minute. At sea level, 10 lbs of air per minute equals 130 cu. ft/min. At 20,000 ft., 10 lbs of air per minute equals 245 c. ft./min.
Method of Heat Transference	The two methods of heat transfer from one substance to another are conduction and radiation. Convection, commonly considered to be a method of heat transfer, is actually a method of heat movement within the substance.
Molecule	The smallest particle of a substance that can exist and still retain all of the characteristics of that substance.
Momentum	Then tendency of a body to continue after being placed in motion.
Net Thrust	The effective thrust developed by the engine during a flight taking into consideration the initial momentum of the air mass before entering the engine.
Over speed	RPM in excess of design 100% RPM.
Over temp	The temperature in excess of the maximum allowable design temperature at the turbine exit.
Power	The rate of doing work. Work per unit of time.
Power Lever	The cockpit lever that connects to the fuel control unit for scheduling fuel flow to the combustor. Also called power control lever or throttle.
Power Turbine	A turbine rotor connected to an output reduction gearbox. Also referred to as a free power turbine.
Pressure	This can be defined as force per unit area, eg. Total Force divided by the effective area = pressure. If total force is measured in pounds and effective area is measured in square inches, the pressure would be expressed as pounds per square inch (PSI).
Pressure Altitude	A pressure expressed in feet, equal to barometric pressure (absolute) at the stated altitude, i.e. a 10,000 foot pressure altitude is equivalent to 20.58 "Hg A (10.11 PSIA) regardless of its actual location, since 20.58 "Hg A is the pressure at 10,000 feet in a standard atmosphere. The higher the pressure altitude, in feet, the lower the pressure in inches Hg A.
Pressure Drop	The difference in pressure between two points, that results from resistance to flow between these points. These points may be across a heat exchanger, upstream and downstream in a duct, etc.
Probe	A sensing device that extends into the airstream or gas stream for measuring pressure. In the case of pressure, it is used to measure total pressure.
Propulsive Efficiency	The external efficiency of an engine expressed as a percentage.
Ram	The amount of pressure build-up above ambient at the engine's compressor inlet, due to the forward motion of the engine through the air. (Air's initial momentum.)
Ram Pressure Rise	The pressure rise in the inlet due to the forward speed of the aircraft, e.g. at M = .85 a pressure rise of 1.6 times above ambient will typically occur.
Ram Ratio	The ratio of ram pressure to ambient pressure.
Ram Recovery	The ability of an engine's air inlet duct to take advantage of Ram.

Term	Definition
Ram Temperature	The temperature of the ambient air plus the ram temperature rise.
Ram Temperature Rise	The ram temperature rise is a function of speed and altitude. The increase in temperature is created by air compression on the exposed surfaces of an object travelling through the atmosphere.
S.A.E.	Society of Automotive Engineers
Sensible Heat	The heat that causes a temperature change when added to or removed from matter. Temperature changes that are apparent to the senses and may be measured.
Shock Stall	Turbulent airflow on an aerofoil which occurs when the speed of sound is reached. The shock wave distorts the aerodynamic airflow, causing a stall and loss of lift.
Shroud	A cover or housing used to aid in confining an air gas flow to a desired path.
Single-Spool Compressor	A single axial flow compressor design, typically with eight or more stages.
Sonic Speed	The speed of sound at ambient or local conditions.
Specific Heat of a Substance	A relative figure derived from the amount of heat required (BTUs) to raise the temperature of one pound of the substance as compared to one pound of water.
Speed of Sound	The terminal velocity of sound waves in air at a specific air temperature. Referred to as Mach 1. The symbol is M.
Static Pressure	The pressure measured in a duct containing air, a gas or a liquid in which no velocity (ram) pressure is allowed to enter the measuring device. Symbol is P_S.
Subsonic Speed	Speed less than that of sound.
Superheat	The temperature of gas above that of the boiling point of its liquid state, i.e. steam 217°F (103°C) at one-atmosphere pressure is superheated 5°F, because water boils at 212°F (100°C) at one atmosphere of pressure.
Supersonic Speed	Speed in excess of sound.
Static Thrust	The thrust developed by an engine, without any initial air mass momentum present due to the engine's static condition.
Temperature Drop	The decrease in temperature for any reason. Temperature drop may occur across a turbine, be due to radiation, heat losses in a duct, etc.
Temperature	The temperature of a body is a measure of how hot or cold the body is, i.e. the heat intensity or heat concentration in the matter.
Thermal Efficiency	Internal engine efficiency or fuel energy available versus work produced, expressed as a percentage.
Thrust	A pushing force exerted by one mass against another, that tends to produce motion in the masses. In jet propulsion, thrust is the forward force in the direction of motion caused by the pressure forces acting on the inner surfaces of the engine. Or, in other words, it is the reaction to the exhaust gases exiting the nozzle. Thrust force is generally measured in pounds or kilograms.
Thrust Specific Fuel Consumption (TSFC)	The weight of fuel in pounds that the engine must burn per hour to generate one pound of thrust.

Term	Definition
Torque	A force, multiplied by its lever arm, acting at right angles to an axis.
Total Pressure	Static Pressure plus ram pressure. Total pressure can be measured by using a specially shaped probe that stops a small portion of the gas or liquid flowing in a duct thereby changing velocity (ram) energy to pressure energy. The symbol is P_t.
Transient Conditions	Conditions that may occur briefly while accelerating or decelerating, or while passing through a specific range of engine operation.
Turbine Stage	A stage that consists of a turbine stator vane set followed by a turbine rotor blade set.
Vector	A line which, by scaled length, indicates magnitude, and whose arrowhead represents the direction of action.
Velocity	The actual change of distance with respect to time. The average velocity is equal to the total distance divided by the total time. Usually expressed in mph or fps.
Work	A force acting through a distance. W = F x D.

Bibliography

Please find below citations to books, websites or images that were referenced during the authoring of this book.

Allproducts.com, online image viewed 21 November 2013, http://www.allproducts.com/manufacture97/jaff/product4.html

Apportioning the airflow – Combustion Process, visited 9 February 2014. http://aeromodelbasic.blogspot.com.au/2011/12/apportioning-airflow-combustion-process.html

Army, U S, and N. Ean. 2001. *Rotary Wing Flight*: Aviation Supplies & Academics, Incorporated.

ASC, AVGAS identification label, viewed 14 November 2013, >http://www.asearle.co.uk/AVGAS-fuel-testing.html<

ASC, Jet A-1 identification label, viewed 14 November 2013, >http://www.asearle.co.uk/JetA1.html<

Avery, R. 1998. Basic Gas Turbine Texts for Pilots: A Self Study Course: Avfacts ATPL Training.

Bell Textron. Bell 206B Flight Manual.

CASA, Gas Turbine Power Plants Text 6.

Corporation, United Technologies, Pratt, and Whitney. 1988. *The Aircraft Gas Turbine Engine and Its Operation*: United Technologies [with] Pratt & Whitney.

Frank Whittle demonstrating first jet engine, 1937 by Rod Lovesy, online image viewed 21 November 2013, http://www.midlandairmuseum.co.uk/jet.php

Inside a turbocharger, Image courtesy Garrett, online image viewed 21 November 2013, http://www.howstuffworks.com/turbo2.htm

Introduction – An early combustion chamber. Visited 9 February 2014. http://aeromodelbasic.blogspot.com.au/2011/12/introduction-early-combustion-chamber.html

Jack Snell, Foter.com, CC BY-ND, Pratt & Whitney R-4360 Wasp Major Radial Engine Cutaway 3, viewed 21 November 2013, > http://foter.com/f/photo/6819832398/3f2e364c16/<

Juandesant, Foter.com, CC BY-SA, Antonov III (Engine|Turbofan), viewed 21 November 2013, > http://foter.com/photo/antonov-iii-engine-turbofan/<

Labyrinth Seal, Picsbox.biz, online image viewed 21 November 2013, http://picsbox.biz/key/labyrinth%20seal%20animation

Little Henry, Aerofiles.com, viewed 21 November 2013, http://www.aerofiles.com/mcdon-79.jpg

Lycoming. Alison / Lycoming notes.

McDonnell, XH-20, Little Henry, Flikr.com, No known copyright restrictions exist, viewed 21 November 2013, <http://www.flickr.com/photos/sdasmarchives/4561398595/in/photostream/<

Otis, C.E., and P.A. Vosbury. 2002. *Aircraft Gas Turbine Powerplants Workbook*: Jeppesen Sanderson.

Royce, Rolls. 1966. *The Jet Engine. 2. Ed*: Rolls-Royce.

RR250-MTU-C20B, MTU Aero Engines, viewed 21 November 2013, http://www.mtu.de/en/products_services/military_business/programs/rr250_c20/index.html

Schafer, J.A. 2007. *Helicopter Maintenance*: Jeppesen.

Service, United States. Flight Standards. 1978. *Basic Helicopter Handbook*: Department of Transportation, Federal Aviation Administration, Flight Standards Service.

Texas Oil Seals.com, online image viewed 21 November 2013, http://www.texasoilseals.com/PTFE%20OIL%20SEALS.html

Tony in WA, Foter.com, CC BY-SA, Pratt & Whitney JT9D, viewed 21 November 2013, > http://foter.com/f/photo/3613338204/5ddf811b80/<

Basic Gas Turbines *for Helicopter Pilots*

Turbine Labyrinth Seal, PP Engineering and Pattern Industries, online image viewed 21 November 2013, http://www.indiamart.com/ppengineering/steam-turbine-parts.html

Turbine Services Limited, online image viewed 21 November 2013, http://www.turbineservices.com/researchDesignBuild.php

Wild, Kroes. Aircraft Power Plants.

Woodhouse, Mark. Basic Gas Turbine Knowledge.

Image References and Attributions

[1] Frank Whittle demonstrating first jet engine, 1937 by Rod Lovesy, online image viewed 21 November 2013, http://www.midlandairmuseum.co.uk/jet.php

[2] Jack Snell, Foter.com, CC BY-ND, Pratt & Whitney R-4360 Wasp Major Radial Engine Cutaway 3, viewed 21 November 2013, > http://foter.com/f/photo/6819832398/3f2e364c16/<

[3] Tony in WA, Foter.com, CC BY-SA, Pratt & Whitney JT9D, viewed 21 November 2013, > http://foter.com/f/photo/3613338204/5ddf811b80/<

[4] McDonnell, XH-20, Little Henry, wikipedia.org, public domain, viewed 21 November 2013, https://en.wikipedia.org/wiki/McDonnell_XH-20_Little_Henry#/media/File:McDonnell_XH-20_in_flight.jpg

[5] Army XH-26 Pulse Jet Helicopter, Harry S. Truman Library Museum, public domain, https://www.trumanlibrary.gov/photograph-records/63-1387-03

[6] Juandesant, Foter.com, CC BY-SA, Antonov III (Engine|Turbofan), viewed 21 November 2013, > http://foter.com/photo/antonov-iii-engine-turbofan/<

[7] RR250-MTU-C20B, MTU Aero Engines, viewed 21 November 2013, http://www.mtu.de/en/products_services/military_business/programs/r-250_c20/index.html

[8] Introduction – An early combustion chamber. Visited 9 February 2014. http://aeromodelbasic.blogspot.com.au/2011/12/introduction-early-combustion-chamber.html

[9] Apportioning the airflow – Combustion Process, visited 9 February 2014. http://aeromodelbasic.blogspot.com.au/2011/12/apportioning-airflow-combustion-process.html

[10] Martin Brown, picryl.com, public domain, accessed 09/02/2022, https://picryl.com/media/burner-rig-showing-specimens-rotating-and-not-rotating-utility-turbine-blade-0d50bf?action=upgrade

[11] Labyrinth Seal, Picsbox.biz, online image viewed 21 November 2013, http://picsbox.biz/key/labyrinth%20seal%20animation

[12] Turbine Labyrinth Seal, PP Engineering and Pattern Industries, online image viewed 21 November 2013, http://www.indiamart.com/ppengineering/steam-turbine-parts.html

[13] Allproducts.com, online image viewed 21 November 2013, http://www.allproducts.com/manufacture97/jaff/product4.html

[14] Texas Oil Seals.com, online image viewed 21 November 2013, http://www.texasoilseals.com/PTFE%20OIL%20SEALS.html

[15] Turbine Services Limited, online image viewed 21 November 2013, http://www.turbineservices.com/researchDesignBuild.php

Index

A

accessory drive section 64
AD
   lubricants 88
aeolipile
   history 6
aero-thermodynamic duct 12
Agusta 109
   intake 27
air intake 27
air intake and filters
   fixed wing 27
   helicopters 27
airflow
   axial flow compressor 39
airflow control
   axial flow compressor 40
annular
   combustion chamber 52
anticipator cable
   governor 75
anti-ice system
   compressor 43
ashless dispersant
   engine oil 88
athodyd 12
automatic governor
   governor 75
AVTUR
   fuel type 82
axial flow
   compressor 30
   stagger angle 38
axial flow compressor
   compressor section 35

B

B206
   beep control governor 75
   governor 76
   linear actuator 76
battery
   starter motor 97
beep control
   governor 75
beep governor
   governor 75
bendix system
   starter system 96
blade attachment
   turbine blade 59
blade materials
   turbine blade 60
blade shrouds
   turbine blade 59
bleed air
   axial flow compressor 43
bleed air valve
   axial flow compressor 41
boyles law
   gas laws 10
   how a turbine works 24
branca
   history 6
brayton cycle
   turbine engine 22
   turbine jet 14
brush seals
   turbine engine sealing 95
buzz bomb 12
bypass system
   intake filter 28

C

can
   combustion chamber 51
can-annular
   combustion chamber 52
carbon seals
   turbine engine sealing 95
cascade effect
   axial flow compressor 35
CCA
   starter battery 97
CECO
   starter system 97
centrifugal compressor
   axial flow compressor 39
   compressor section 32
centrifugal flow
   compressor 30
Chandler Evans Company
   starter system 97
charles law
   how a turbine works 24
charles laws
   gas laws 10
chemical stability
   oil properties 89
chip detector
   lubrication system 93
chip plug
   lubrication system 93
cleans
   oil functions 87
cold cranking amps
   starter battery 97
colour
   fuel 82
combination
   turbine cooling 63
combined axial
   axial flow compressor 39
combined gas law
   gas laws 11
combustion assembly 49
combustion chamber
   types 51
combustion section 48
compatibility
   engine oil 88
components
   ignition system 98
   lubrication system 91
   starter system 97
compression stall
   remedy 46
compressor rotor blade attachment 37
compressor section 30
compressor stall

Basic Gas Turbines *for Helicopter Pilots*

```
        damage ................................................................ 47
        symptoms ............................................................ 46
compressor stalls
        axial flow compressor ........................................ 44
compressor surge
        symptoms ............................................................ 46
compressor surging
        axial flow compressor ........................................ 44
contamination
        turbine fuel .......................................................... 86
convection
        turbine cooling .................................................... 62
convergent ducting ................................................... 26
cooling
        oil functions ........................................................ 87
        turbine section .................................................... 62
corncob ........................................................................ 7
corrosion
        oil functions ........................................................ 87
creep
        turbine blade ...................................................... 60
critical icing temperature
        fuel ....................................................................... 85
D
data acquisition unit
        fuel control ......................................................... 77
DAU
        fuel control systems .......................................... 77
de-aerator
        lubrication system .............................................. 91
decibels
        exhaust section .................................................. 68
diffuser
        compressor section ........................................... 34
dipstick
        lubrication system .............................................. 91
dissolved water
        water in turbine fuel ........................................... 84
divergent ducting ...................................................... 26
double entry
        impeller ............................................................... 33
**dovetail root** ............................................................. **37**
ducted fan .................................................................. 15
ducting
        turbine engine ..................................................... 26
duplex
        fuel spray ............................................................ 79
E
EEC
        fuel control systems .......................................... 77
electric fuel boost pump
        fuel control ......................................................... 69
electronic engine control
        fuel control ......................................................... 77
engine driven fuel pump
        fuel control ......................................................... 70
engine fuel
        turbine ................................................................. 81
engine oil
        properties ........................................................... 89
        turbine engines ................................................... 89
        types .................................................................... 88
engine oil types
        lubrication ........................................................... 88
engine relight
        starting problems ............................................. 101
engine sealing
        turbine ................................................................. 94
engine seals
        types .................................................................... 94
engine shutdown
        starting problems ............................................. 101
```

```
exhaust section ........................................................ 66
F
faced pads
        accessory drive .................................................. 64
FADEC
        fuel control systems .......................................... 77
        starter system .................................................... 96
FAFC
        fuel control systems .......................................... 77
FCU
        fuel control ......................................................... 71
FFR
        fuel control systems .......................................... 77
filters ........................................................................... 27
fine wire gauze filter
        intake filters ........................................................ 28
**fir-tree root** ............................................................. **37**
fixed turbine .............................................................. 19
fixed wing
        air intake and filters ........................................... 27
flame out
        combustion ......................................................... 51
        starting problems ............................................. 101
flash point
        oil properties ...................................................... 89
FMU
        fuel control systems .......................................... 77
FOD
        intake filter ......................................................... 28
forces
        turbine blade ...................................................... 59
foreign object damage
        intake filter ......................................................... 28
**formula**
        **charles law** ................................................ **10**, **11**
free turbine ............................................................... 19
free water
        water in turbine fuel ........................................... 84
friction
        oil functions ........................................................ 87
FSII
        fuel icing ............................................................. 86
fuel
        colour .................................................................. 82
        contamination ..................................................... 86
        critical icing temperature ................................... 85
        fungus ................................................................. 86
        test kit ................................................................. 85
fuel characteristics
        turbine engine fuel ............................................. 82
fuel control systems
        turbine engine .................................................... 69
fuel control unit
        fuel control ......................................................... 71
fuel flow regulator
        fuel control ......................................................... 77
fuel pump
        electric ................................................................. 69
        engine driven ...................................................... 70
        plunger ................................................................ 70
        positive displacement ........................................ 70
fuel spray nozzle
        fuel control ......................................................... 78
fuel spray pattern .................................................... 78
fuel types
        turbine engine .................................................... 81
full authority digital engine control
        fuel control ......................................................... 77
full authority fuel control
        fuel control ......................................................... 77
full flow system
        lubrication system .............................................. 91
fungus
```

fuel 86
G
gas flow
   exhaust section 67
gas laws
   jet propulsion 10
gas producer turbine 55
   compressor 30
   turbine 55
gas turbine
   history 7
gasolene
   fuel type 81
gay-lussac's law
   gas laws 10
gear pump
   oil pump 92
governors
   fuel control 71, 75
grades
   oil properties 89
H
harness
   ignition components 99
heating systems
   water in turbine fuel 86
helicopters
   air intake and filters 27
high bypass 16
   turbofan 15
history 6
hot shutdown
   starting problems 102
hot starts
   starting problems 100
hung starts
   starting problems 100
hydraulic seals
   turbine engine sealing 95
I
IBF
   intake filter 29
ice
   water in turbine fuel 85
icing inhibitor
   water in turbine fuel 86
igniter box
   ignition components 99
   ignition system 98
igniter leads
   ignition components 99
igniter plug
   ignition components 98
ignition
   turbine engine 96
ignition system
   turbine engine 98
impeller
   compressor section 33
   double entry 33
   single entry 33
impulse turbine blade 57
inlet barrier
   intake filters 28
inlet barrier filter
   intake filter 29
inlet guide vanes 33
intake design
   air intake and filters 27
intake filters
   air intake and filters 28
intake ice
   air intake and filters 28

internal air
   turbine cooling 62
J
jet fuel
   types 82
jet propulsion
   basic principles 9
Jet Ranger
   anti-ice switch **43**
   electric pumps 69
   intake 27
L
labyrinth seals
   turbine engine sealing 94
low bypass 16
   turbofan 15
lubrication
   turbine engine 87
lubrication system 90
   turbine engine 90
M
manifold
   compressor section 34
mechanical energy
   turbine fuel 81
metallic ash detergent
   engine oil 88
mixing oils **88**
modulated
   starter system 96
multiple-can
   combustion chamber 51
N
N1
   compressor 30
   fuel control 73
   turbine 55
N1 topping
   compressor 46
N2
   fuel control 73
   turbine 55
newton
   jet propulsion 9
NGVs
   turbine section 56
noise levels
   exhaust section 68
noise suppression
   exhaust section 68
nozzle guide vanes
   turbine 55
   turbine section 56
O
oil
   functions 87
oil cooler
   lubrication system 91
oil filter
   lubrication system 91
oil pump
   lubrication system 92
oil tank
   lubrication system 91
oils
   mixing **88**
P
particle separator
   intake filters 28
particle separators
   intake filters 28
petrol
   fuel type 81

Basic Gas Turbines *for Helicopter Pilots*

piston engine
- replacement 7

plumbing
- fuel control 80
- lubrication system 92

pour point
- oil properties 89

power turbine 56
- turbine 55

pressure
- turbine engine 24

pressure changes
- turbine engine 24

pressure ratio
- compressor section 32

pressure relief valve system
- lubrication system 91

pressure relief valves
- lubrication system 92

primary air
- combustion 50

prop fan 18

properties
- engine oil 89

PRV
- lubrication system 91

pulse-jet
- jet propulsion 12

R

R-4360 7

ram-jet
- jet propulsion 12

rattle
- turbine 59

reaction principle
- jet propulsion 9

reaction turbine blade 58

rear fan 18

re-circulatory system
- lubrication system 90

retaining pin 37

ring seals
- turbine engine sealing 95

rocket jet
- jet propulsion 11

Rolls Royce (Allison)
- compressor 32
- turbine engine 24, 25

Rolls Royce 250C20
- turbine 55

Rolls Royce C20
- air flow 39
- compressor 39

Rolls Royce C250C20
- accessory drive 65

rotating turbine
- turbine 55
- turbine section 57

rotor blade attachment
- compressor 37

rotor blades
- axial flow compressor 37

S

sand filter
- intake filters 28

Saybolt Second Universal
- lubricants 89

Saybolt Universal Viscosimeter
- lubricants 89

scavenge pump
- lubrication system 90

sealing
- turbine engine 94

seals
- types 94

secondary air
- combustion 50

shaft horse power
- turbine 54

shear point
- oil pump 92

shutdown
- starting problems 101
- turbine engine 96

simplex
- fuel spray 79

single entry
- impeller 33

Squirrel AS350
- chip plug 93

SSU
- lubricants 89

stagger angle
- axial flow compressor 38

starter motor
- starter components 97

starter system
- turbine engine 96

starting
- turbine engine 96

starting problems
- turbine engine 100

stator blades 37

stator row 37

stator vanes
- axial flow compressor 38

steam turbine
- history 6

straight mineral
- engine oil 88

stretching
- turbine blades 60

surface film
- turbine cooling 62

suspended water
- water in turbine fuel 83

swirl vanes 33
- combustion 50

synthetic
- engine oil 88

T

temperature
- turbine engine 24

temperature changes
- turbine engine 25

test kit
- fuel 85

testing for water
- water in turbine fuel 85

third law of physics
- reaction principle 9

throttle
- fuel control 73

turbine
- cooling 62

turbine blade
- forces 59

turbine blade types
- turbine section 57

turbine engine 7
- advantages 8
- how it works 21
- ignition 96
- lubrication system 90
- shutdown 96

starting 96
turbine engine fuel 81
turbine engine lubrication 87
turbine engine sealing 94
turbine engines
    oil 89
turbine fuel
    characteristics 82
    water 83
turbine jet
    jet propulsion 14
turbine section 54
turbo fans
    turbine jet 14
turbo jet
    brayton cycle 23
    history 7
    turbine jet 14
turboprops
    turbine jet 18
turboshaft
    turbine jet 20

two stage compressor 33
V
variable inlet guide vanes
    axial flow compressor 40
variable stator vanes
    axial flow compressor 41
velocity
    turbine engine 24
viscosity
    oil properties 89
volume
    turbine engine 24
volume changes
    turbine engine 24
W
water
    turbine engine fuel 83
wet start
    starting problems 100
whittle
    history 7

www.ingramcontent.com/pod-product-compliance
Lightning Source LLC
Chambersburg PA
CBHW042017090526
44588CB00024B/2886